Farming
with
Raymond

Farming

with

Raymond

But I Never Milked a Cow

CM Mary

FARMING WITH RAYMOND
BUT I NEVER MILKED A COW

Author Credits: Constance M Milz

iUniverse books may be ordered through booksellers or by contacting:

iUniverse
1663 Liberty Drive
Bloomington, IN 47403
www.iuniverse.com
1-800-Authors (1-800-288-4677)

Because of the dynamic nature of the Internet, any web addresses or links contained in this book may have changed since publication and may no longer be valid. The views expressed in this work are solely those of the author and do not necessarily reflect the views of the publisher, and the publisher hereby disclaims any responsibility for them.

Any people depicted in stock imagery provided by Getty Images are models, and such images are being used for illustrative purposes only.
Certain stock imagery © Getty Images.

ISBN: 978-1-5320-6826-3 (sc)
ISBN: 978-1-5320-6827-0 (e)

Library of Congress Control Number: 2019901408

Print information available on the last page.

iUniverse rev. date: 02/08/19

Farming
with
Raymond

But I Never Milked a Cow

CM Mary

FARMING WITH RAYMOND
BUT I NEVER MILKED A COW

Author Credits: Constance M Milz

iUniverse books may be ordered through booksellers or by contacting:

iUniverse
1663 Liberty Drive
Bloomington, IN 47403
www.iuniverse.com
1-800-Authors (1-800-288-4677)

ISBN: 978-1-5320-6826-3 (sc)
ISBN: 978-1-5320-6827-0 (e)

Library of Congress Control Number: 2019901408

Print information available on the last page.

iUniverse rev. date: 02/08/19

If you see CM Mary, also known as my sister Connie Milz, she probably has a journal in her hand or in the bag she is carrying. This is because she is always doing research or looking for ideas for her next book. She does enjoy reading as well as writing and if she asks you to repeat something, be cautious because it might end up in a book as a direct quote or in some work of fiction. In this book, she tells you about her life being married to a dairy farmer with some humorous attempts on helping with the farm. Our father will attest to the difficulty of having inexperienced help on a farm with having three girls as helpers before a boy came along. I hope you enjoy this latest book about my sister's life as a dairy farmer's wife who never milked a cow.

Patricia Sauber
CM Mary's younger sister

PROLOGUE

It was my sister-in-law Cindy Milz that came up with the subtitle for this book. When she heard that I was writing about my experience as a farm wife, she felt it needed to be said that while I may have helped on the farm, "I never milked a cow." As you read my book, you will understand it was better that way because Raymond and I each had separate careers and interests. We like to believe that is why we get along so good. The chapters follow the events in our lives together, but I might not have everything in perfect chronological order. If I decided this work had to be perfect before it was published, I would never be able to share my story. The picture on the front cover demonstrates what I contribute to the farm. Raymond used it to store corn, but I call it my gazebo.

CHAPTER ONE

"In every job that must be done, there is an element of fun."
Mary Poppins

Raymond worked in a factory in Colby, Wisconsin when we were first married in July of 1970. I always knew he wanted to farm and I had lived in the country all my life except for the four years I spent in college from September of 1966 to June of 1970. Guess I thought that my life in the country wouldn't change much when I married this guy from Loyal, Wisconsin. I had no idea what I was getting myself into when I married a man that wanted to be a dairy farmer. I guess some would say that I was living under a box of rocks because when my family moved to Wisconsin to live on a dairy farm, I should have been able to realize all the work that goes into that occupation. My first story should explain what a sheltered life I lived. When I was in college at Northern Illinois University, another student asked me if it was true that cows would be bred every year to produce a calf and milk. Understanding only the reproductive system of humans made me think that the idea might be right. After checking with my father, I just had to wonder when I would have ever learned about that side of milking cows if I had not gone to college to become a Physical Education teacher. To improve my prospects of getting a job, I added minors in Health and Driver Education. While those degrees did help me get a job, they didn't help with my knowledge of the dairy farming business.

Just before I entered college, I went with Grandpa and Grandma Schmitt to visit my cousin, Jerry McDonald who was in the seminary studying to be a Capuchin priest. He had taken the name Father Barnabas at the time. During our visit, we were introduced to another priest, and he asked me if I didn't think I should pursue a more challenging degree instead of Physical Education. He obviously didn't know about the science and biology needed for my intended degree. Father Barnabas came to my defense by saying, "She is a farmer's daughter, and I think she is in the right place." He was a wise cousin.

In June of 1970 when I completed college, it was time to both get a job and plan a wedding. Back in the 70's, I didn't need to do all that seems necessary today when planning a wedding. Pew bows and table favors were not needed at the time. I remember a parish priest telling me there is no reason to decorate the church any more than on a regular Sunday. He felt it was always ready to honor the Lord. Father Barnabas was the priest that married us. He had been a Capuchin priest for about ten years, and every time we saw each other at a family reunion in later years, he would ask if we were still married. After the wedding, while I was thanking him for the beautiful service, he asked if I would like a copy of his sermon. Sounded like a great idea because I might not have heard all of it at the time of the delivery. He sent me a copy which I have read many times since then, and I always get something out of it. I included the text here for your review.

"Very little need be said on an occasion such as this. After all what is important this morning is not what I am going to say, but rather what this couple is doing. At times we are unimpressed by words, but actions are always impressive. Therefore the sermon of today's liturgy is not my words, but rather what Raymond and Connie are doing. All that is necessary for me to do is to clarify and make more understandable the meaning of their actions.

What they are telling us this morning can be stated simply in these words: 'If one wishes to come into the fullness of his life, he must do so through love.'

Long before Raymond met Connie, he had dreams about his life. I'm sure, like every young man, he envisioned the day when he would be a father and have a home of his own and show his love through the support he would bring to his wife and his children. I'm sure that Connie too, long before she met Raymond, had much the same dreams. One day she would be a mother; she too would have a home of her own and with tender devotion she would care for her husband and her children.

But then as they both grew to maturity, they began to realize that their dreams were built on a condition. Their dreams would come true only if they found someone whom they could truly love and who could return that love.

It was God who took care of this condition. It was He who placed in the hearts of Connie and Raymond a love for one another. And in giving Connie to Raymond, He bestowed upon him the rest of his life. Likewise, in giving Raymond to Connie, He bestowed upon her the rest of her life. Each now was to find in the other a fullness of life which would have been impossible before.

This morning as Raymond and Connie publicly profess and confirm that love, let us take to heart what they are telling us. If we are to enter the fullness of our lives, we too must do so though love. It is a message for all of us. For those of you who are looking forward to the day of your own marriage, they point out the necessity of learning who to truly love. For those of you who are already married, they point out that the greater love you bring to your married life, the fuller it will be. Even for me, a celibate priest, they have a message: If I wish to come into the fullness of my priesthood, I can only do so by opening my heart to all who come to me.

Yes, their message is for us all. A simple message which summarizes all that Christ taught: If you wish to enter into the fullness of life, the gateway is love!"

Again, I have to say what a wise cousin I had. He was an incredible individual. We received a note from the seminary where Father Jerry was living at the time of his death. He didn't live long enough to see Raymond and I celebrate twenty-five years together. He is missed.

My wedding dress was borrowed from a college friend, I stood up in her wedding the year before mine, and she gave me her dress after the ceremony. The price was right; it was a beautiful dress, so why not use it. My future sister-in-law, Pat Lang altered the dress for a perfect fit. My mother made two of the three dresses needed for my bridal party for my sisters Patricia and Pamela who were in my wedding. The third attendant was Ray's sister Beverly and again Pat's skills as a seamstress were employed because she made Bev's dress. We were married at St. Anthony's Catholic Church in Loyal, Wisconsin on July 25th. Raymond will tell you it was a very hot day, but I don't remember it being so uncomfortable. Our reception and meal were at Mom and Dad's farm with a dance that night in Rozellville.

We made our first home in Abbotsford where we lived in a second-floor apartment. I don't recall what we paid for rent, but the landlord gave us a discount on the cost each month because Ray mowed the lawn when needed and shoveled snow in the winter. He was working a swing shift at the local box factory, and I was teaching in Marshfield. But he had plans to save some money to start farming. Thus we were in Abbotsford for only ten months during which time we saved my salary and lived on what he made. While in Abbotsford we joined St. James parish; which was the first official parish that Ray and I attended as husband and wife. We were able to go to Mass most of the time together. On All Saints Day, November 1, 1970, we went to an evening Mass for the holy day of obligation, only to find out that the 8 pm service was the night before; we were just twenty-four hours late. As we headed home to "satisfy our obligation" we decided to say a rosary. I was leading the prayer so when my mother called, I answer with "Hail Mary" instead of "hello." Because my mother's name is Mary, she was confused until I explained what we were doing. Here I will have to tell you a story about my mother-in-law, Luella, as long as I have mentioned my Mom. One of the first nights we stayed overnight at Luella's she was up to "no good." When we got in bed, the sheets were clean, but "short-sheeted." As I recall it was her idea, but the person that did the work was her daughter Beverly.

When we found a place to rent in Arpin our savings account didn't go very far, but we went to the bank for a loan. We were able to start farming on a rented place with less than twenty thousand dollars of debt. It has to be mentioned that Ray was told by more that one person not to try to farm on the place we signed to rent for three years. We didn't listen, and we could buy enough cows and machinery to start farming. It was back in the 1970's when a person could still afford to get into Ray's profession. We moved to Arpin in April 1970, but there were no cows until May 20th. Raymond had lots to do to prepare the barn for his cows. There were always stanchions to be fixed and water cups to be replaced or repaired. He remembers the gutter was frozen, so the barn cleaner had to be thawed to free it and get it working. His first fourteen cows came from Thorp, and he got three from Granton. Anytime you are riding in the countryside with Raymond, and you pass a farm where he purchased cows, machinery, or feed; he'll remind you. Because of that fact, I should know what farm they were from, but it just isn't that high on my priority list to keep all that information in my brain. I do remember where another ten cows were purchased. They came from the John Hollar farm in Milladore. I'll explain later why I can remember those ten cows without much effort.

Things were different back then because prices were lower as well as the wages. But not as low as I assumed when I think back to how we met our first banker in Arpin. Raymond had paid the feed bill using a check but forgot to record it in the register. He asked me to do it for him and said he had made the check out for "two fifty." Does "two fifty" mean $2.50 or $250? I recorded it as two dollars and fifty cents which was too low for any kind of feed purchased. It was about three weeks later when he went to purchase a cow for $900, thinking he had plenty of money, because of that $247.50 mistake. The account was overdrawn, and we didn't have a lot in the savings account, so Glenn Hartman, our personal banker, decided to stop by and introduce himself to Raymond. That was the beginning of a wonderful relationship but more about Hartman's later.

But let's go back to my job. Just before we were married, I was hired as a Physical Education teacher at the high school in Marshfield. During the summer of 1970, Russ Knapp had interviewed and hired at least four new female teachers thinking they were all single. Imagine his surprise when we started and all of us were married or engaged by that September. None of us were from the same college, but all of us understood that when we were interviewing it was best not to flash an engagement ring. I know I took my ring off for the interview and didn't mention my wedding coming up that July. The reason to conceal an engagement was that it was thought that a woman might follow her husband to another job meaning the teaching position would be open in a few years if not the very next year. When the dust finally settled, I was at Marshfield for thirty-three years, and during those years I only had a twenty-minute drive to work and Raymond had a sixty-second walk.

One of the first tractors Raymond purchased was a 4-Star Moline which ran on LP gas. This tractor used a very unusual type of fuel, so for that reason, we were able to get the tractor for less money. We had to get a tank for the LP gas which was done, and we owned our big tractor which was sixty horse. That term "sixty horse" means in theory that our tractor had the same amount of power as sixty real horses. One weekend when he headed to the barn, I headed to the field using that tractor to disc. Apparently, as I came off the road to head down in the field, I hit both of the brakes to slow up. Hitting both brakes at the same time set the brakes, which I didn't realize. Later when Raymond came to the field to check on me, he could smell something burning. I had been discing for over an hour with those brakes set or locked. Raymond asked why I had not noticed that the tractor was working hard. It never occurred to me that the tractor was working hard because it seems like they always do work hard. Think about sixty horses pulling a disc, that is hard work. As far as the smell; I figured it would go away or maybe that was how tractors smell when they are working hard. Not sure what happened next but I do know the brakes were never the best on that tractor. Please understand, at that point in my life, I had limited experience in the art of driving a tractor. But if a tractor can pull a disc with the brakes locked, I don't believe the brakes were very good before I started that day, and they were not worth much when the day ended.

It has to be said that Raymond is the calmer of the two of us. He seldom gets upset and raises his voice, but he can. Once he did when I went to a field to get a wagon for him to fill with feed for our cattle to eat. As I came up out of the field, the wagon pulled in two. I was pulling the front half of the wagon with the other half still in the field. Instead of pulling only half a wagon back to the yard, I unhooked it on the side of the road and headed home to tell Raymond. His exact words were, "Well if you wouldn't drive like a bat out of ***, it wouldn't pull apart." Now I don't handle criticism well. So I'm not sure why, but I continued to do my chores in the barn that morning, and before they were completed he came back to explain that the main bolt in the middle of the wagon was rusty, which was why it broke and now I could help him get it back together. I refused and told him to get his buddy, Arnie. This was Arnie Ellis, a neighbor that Raymond worked with when he needed a little extra help. Yes, Raymond did apologize, but that was after he had gotten help from Arnie and realized that he needed to use Arnie's loader which is mounted on a tractor to lift the wagon parts to get them back together. We didn't own a loader at the time, and it took more skill than I had to get the wagon fixed, so it was a good thing Arnie and Ray worked together. Arnie's wife Joyce, like many farm wives, would do the milking so Arnie could do other things that farmers do. It was interesting that many neighbors that had cows of their own to milk would stop to talk to Ray while he was milking. I asked Ray why this was happening on such a regular basis. He explained that people knew he would be in the barn at milking time and their cows were milked by their wives. Raymond never had the option to not be around at milking time; I never milked a cow. You know what they say about dairy farmers, "They do it twice a day."

Another thing that a farm wife had to do was listen for the phone or wait for a return call. Cell phones make that job obsolete today. Raymond was waiting for the breeder to call back. We used a breeder to inseminate our cows, so we didn't deal with a bull on our farm. Again, it must have been a weekend, and I was in the house cleaning or working on grades, so I was confined to the house which made waiting for a return call easy. Because I was teaching full-time, there was always plenty to do in the house if a person really likes to clean. Let it be said, I like my space clean, but when I clean it I expect it to stay clean. Not a good attitude for a farmer's wife. I was told the breeder was going to call and check on a cow of ours that needed to be bred. Our cows didn't stay in the barn during the day but were turned out between milkings. Ray explained that the cow that needed to be bred was left in the barn. When the call came, the question was, "Is that cow standing?"

"Yes," I explained, "It has been standing in the barn all day."

Because of the short pause and his next comment, which was, "I'll have to talk to Raymond;" I knew I had said something wrong, but it wasn't until Ray told me about the four stages of heat, one of which is referred to as "standing." At some point in my education, I must not have been listening because this was news to me.

Another lesson was if the starter on a tractor isn't working that tractor can be started by being pulled behind another one, and as the speed of the lead tractor is increased the person being pulled just has to pop the clutch, which is letting it out quickly. I was helping Raymond start a tractor using this technique without much success. He was on the lead tractor, and he even tried to switch places with me. Nothing worked so I headed back to my own chores. Within 20 minutes he was back to ask if we could try it again. Who am I to question why it would work this time. Off we went, and as I popped the clutch, it started with the first try. In answer to my raised eyebrows, he told me it works better when the tractor being pulled has gas in it. This same, or should I say similar, lesson can be applied to a truck with a manual transmission. We were trying to start a truck, the same way by him pulling with me following without any success. He stopped to check the gas. Now he was very calm when he explained that we were going to try it once more as he shifted the vehicle into first gear. I had been in reverse. The only thing I have to say is, "it is hard to get good help, and I work cheap!"

Another time when we were trying to start a truck using the method above, when it didn't start on the first try I had learned my lesson and checked to see if I was in reverse. I wasn't in reverse, but we found it was out of gas. That could have been the first truck we purchased. Raymond had to sell his 1964 Ford Galaxy (some spell it Galaxie) 500XL to purchase that old gray truck. He loved that car which was a royal blue with white interior. The truck was a gray color which was a primer and we never did paint it. It was a Ford F150 series, and we don't know the year of the vehicle. It was our first farm truck, served the purpose, and didn't come with payments. Looking back now both of those vehicles would be worth a lot of money but we were focused on farming not collecting vehicles which is a hobby that can cost a lot of money.

I remember Ray sending me to a feed mill in Marshfield to get seed oats using that old gray farm vehicle. Once I was loaded the guy at the feed mill told me to go slow because there was so much weight in the truck bed. Going through town was fine but once on the highway as I increased my speed I had the sensation that the front wheels were not in contact with the road. Needless to say, I slowed down and was passed by every vehicle on the road, but I did make it back to the farm safely. The reason I had that job was because a farmer has chores and can't spend hours on the road while his wife only has a house clean and lesson plans to prepare.

Here we should note that I did help in the barn every morning and evening, but my only purpose was to get in, get it done, and get out. Actually, the only thing I did in the morning was help put the cows in, while in the evening I washed the milkers and fed calves. Only the first time I went out to help at night did I just get up from the table and head to the barn. When we came in I still had the table to clear and dishes to do while Raymond sat down for the night. I asked him about helping me but he explained he had put in a full day. Okay, no argument there, but I had also put in a full day, teaching and making the meal. What I decided that night was in the future I would clean up the table and put away the dishes before going to the barn to help. That way when we came in from the barn we both could sit down and call it a day. Using this technique, we avoided a nightly argument about me doing everything while he just sat. Another time I was able to avoid an argument was the first time Raymond came in from the barn about 5:00 pm, which was when we ate our evening meal. He told me he had not eaten lunch until 3:00 pm or later. The first time this happened, I was angry. But once I calmed down, I realized when that happened I could just eat and put the meal away for the following night. Just change the way you look at things, and it makes for less angry words. What I had to realize was my life at school was defined by bells and a set schedule. Ray's life was set by the cows, the weather, and other people. When he started a project, it had to be finished before going on to the next task. A flat tire on a manure spreader made the task of cleaning the barn longer on any given day. There were big differences in our two jobs.

Not to say I truly understood everything that went into farming. Like the time I was trying to help Raymond start yet another tractor. It was dark, and we were on a gravel road near our farm in Arpin. I was in a truck, and he was hooked behind me in a tractor with a loader on it. The truck was a standard shift, which meant I had to let the clutch out and get to the gas before the chain went slack. The chain between two tractors or vehicles needs to be tight before you start pulling. What was happening was as I let the clutch out Ray would hit me before I could get started. Did I mention we were on a hill? This happened two or three times, and I was getting madder by the second. I came out of that truck screaming like a banshee; to say I was unreasonable would be an understatement. Arnie Ellis arrived about that time because he had seen us on the road. The guys sent me home in Arnie's truck and worked to get the tractor started without my help. As I was driving home, it didn't take me long to realize that Ray wasn't hitting me. As I would let the clutch out the truck would roll backward and hit his tractor. Yes, I felt foolish when I explained to Raymond that I was sorry and just didn't realize what was happening. He didn't actually laugh, but he did have a smirk on his face.

One of the reasons Raymond and I get along so well is because we have separate jobs and responsibilities. We know from experience that if we had worked together one person would have been in charge and the other would need to take and follow directions. The reason I mention this is because of what happened when I tried to organize Raymond's space which was in the barn. I cleaned some shelves for him and tossed items I didn't feel were needed. That was like talking during a weather forecast. A farm wife has a few rules to live by. Never talk while the weather forecast is on the radio or TV and never toss anything away. There is a place for everything, and it will be needed sometime. That last one has been very hard for me. If there is something that I have not used in the last year, except to collect dust, it is time for it to go. That is not true when farming; according to Raymond, a person might need it someday.

As a farm wife going to town every day for work, I realized that I was perfect for the job of gopher. On your lunch can you "Go for this part?" was what my husband said at least once a week. The best was when I was told he had to have the part by the next day and three months later that part was still in the bag. That didn't happen every time. There were times when a piece of machinery was standing in one place, waiting for a part and I was off and running for that part only to return to the farm with the wrong part. I know Raymond would not have come home with the wrong part but I didn't know any better. You have to ask questions before you leave in order to get the right part. What does it do? What tractor is it for? Can I have the old part? Ray did get good at giving me lots of important information as I headed off to pick up parts but often the first question out of the guy's mouth was something I didn't know. Once when I was picking up oil, I took the old container with me so I would come home with the right stuff. I had the right oil, but when Raymond asked for the cost, I showed him the slip. He was so surprised to see that the price had gone up threefold. Just then the company I had been working with called and explained they had charged me too much. That time I headed back to pick up my check and issue another one, and it goes without saying Raymond would have questioned them when they told him the price.

There is a lot to learn on a farm, and I just didn't have my head in the game all the time. I was more concerned about my job. A teacher can move up on the pay scale two ways; complete a year of teaching or take college credits. One of my first years of teaching I took two classes by mail. Because I was a swim coach, I took a swimming class that taught me the basics of each stroke for the purpose of improving a person's time by making their stroke more efficient. I read from the materials, wrote papers, and took a test that was an open book. Keep in mind that all of this work was done on a typewriter. Once the classes were completed, and my grade was received; I turned the information over to the main office and my salary was increased. So in my defense, that is where my head was while Raymond was farming.

There was always an element of fun when Raymond and I were working together. We found it much better to approach each day with some flexibility. This was hard for me because a teacher lives by the clock; actually, it is a bell or tone that moves our day forward. The farmer is controlled by the weather.

CHAPTER TWO

"Fun is good."
Dr. Seuss

At one point in our farming career, we decided it was time to start a family. I have to explain; while I did have a career as a teacher, anyone that has ever been married to a dairy farmer knows farming is also your career. The amount of money needed to farm keeps all individuals engaged in the experience. I knew that I was responsible for half of the debt incurred for this farming venture or should I say adventure? We were not comfortable enough with the income on the farm to decide to give up my teacher's salary but we were ready to start a family. At this point in our careers, we would put half of my teacher's salary, in the savings account and live on the rest. The farm was expected to pay its way; which Raymond, as a good manager was able to make it work. The farm just couldn't purchase additional machinery or new machinery, and that is why the savings account didn't grow as fast as we envisioned. Using the savings account, Raymond planned to farm until it was all gone. Another joke was when the breeder came to the farm and saw something new he would ask, "What did Connie buy you now?" Raymond could have been bothered by these comments, but he took it with a grain of salt and was able to ignore them. He just always paid more than the necessary payment because he had plans to be debt-free someday. At first, he made a double payment until the savings account just couldn't keep up that pace. At one point he was able to reach a happy medium but still always paid more than was required.

During our first summer of farming Ray's sister Nancy, along with her husband David helped us do some baling. That baler was the type that pushes the bale up the chute to be grabbed by someone and stacked on the wagon being pulled behind the baler. Dave's nephew, Lynn Wucherphennig came to work for us that summer. We didn't have an extra bed for him, so Ray went to an auction and purchased one because Lynn was staying with us that night. That major purchase was for one dollar. That bed was around for many years and when it was time to get rid of it I posted a note on Craigslist that said we had a single bed for free. It was gone in less than two hours.

Another thing that Raymond did when we first started farming was work all night long at harvest time. He and Arnie Ellis would work chopping corn all day, taking a break to milk cows at night and then continue working until it was time to milk again in the morning. There would be a huge pile of silage for our cows the next morning that lasted just about to the next harvest season. After doing that just a few times, Raymond decided it wasn't the best idea. Accidents on the farm are common and working 24 hours in one day with no sleep can only increase the possibility. But he had to try it just to say he could do it. For me, it wasn't my favorite activity because I needed my sleep. The house would be open for the guys to come in and warm up while they got something to eat and drink. During one of these all-nighters there was a man knocking on the back door, so I figured, because the door was unlocked, I had to check to see what he wanted. My idea was to meet him at the door instead of giving him an opportunity to walk in the house. The guy was drunk, and his vehicle had run out of gas, so he had walked to town to get some, but as he was walking back, he couldn't find his car. In Arpin where we lived, as a person came out of town, there was a "fork" in the road, so I figured that was where he made his mistake. I used Arnie's truck and took the guy back to his vehicle. I didn't wait to see if he was able to start the car but left him to his own devises. When I got back home, and Raymond heard my story, he was a bit upset that I had helped the guy. I can understand there were many things that could have gone wrong in that scenario, but the guy was little and drunk. I know I could have taken him out if he had tried something. The big issue was that I didn't have my own vehicle; it was the neighbor's, and he was helping us get our work done. The only good thing about this story was my guardian angel was looking over my shoulder.

When we lived on the farm in Arpin, there were plenty of rocks to pick up in all of our fields. During my first year of teaching Raymond came up with the idea of hiring some of my students to help with that task. Because I had all the seniors the first year many of my students could drive and it was easy to find our farm. Rochelle Schalow will remind me anytime she sees me that she was one of those students. Anyone that has ever picked rocks knows it is an experience you don't care to repeat. But if you never have a bad job, you'll never appreciate a good one. So if Rochelle now has a good job she has Raymond to thank.

When we were ready to have our first child, another thing we had to consider was health insurance. My salary was always helpful, but the fact that the farm did not have to provide health insurance for us was a real plus. Another thing that had to be considered was that by teaching one more year; which would have been a total of three years, I was eligible for my lifetime teaching certification. The original plan had been to teach three years, get the life certification and take off to raise the children. The problem with that plan was the job might not be there when it came time to go back to teaching. I also learned that the lifetime certification was only valid if you were teaching. That certification is no longer available today because it was dropped shortly after I received mine. The money to renew a license is a nice income for the state and teachers have to continually take classes to keep their license current. My certification for driver education had to be renewed every three years because that was never part of the lifetime certification.

When I realized I was pregnant, I remember when I told my mother she said I should keep it to myself for a few months and it would make the nine months go by faster. She went on to explain I would get sick of all the questions about how I was feeling and how the pregnancy was going. I didn't listen to her because I was so excited; I told anyone that would listen. My plan was to use her advice when I had the next baby.

It wasn't important to me that I have a boy or a girl; I just asked the Lord for a healthy baby. Valerie Lynn was the answer to that prayer on December 8, 1972. She was due on December 2nd but my sister Pamela had her baby, Jennifer on the first of that month so I went to the hospital to visit my sister and baby on my due date, but my child was going to wait another week. Pam had a due date at the end of December and was thinking she might be in the hospital for Christmas. Babies are full of surprises and come when they are ready.

December 8 is a holy day of obligation in the Catholic Church. On a holy day, you are required or encouraged to attend Mass. The feast day is called the Immaculate Conception which is referring to Mary's conception not Jesus' as some Catholics believe. Raymond and I went to church on the 7th in Arpin because the next evening the Mass would have been in Vesper. After Mass that night there was a social at church, and I mentioned to another woman that I wanted to watch my weight. She told me not to worry about it because I would be getting lots bigger in the next two months. Guess I looked small to her but believe me, I wasn't. My due date had already come and gone; little did I know, but Valerie would be born about 24 hours later.

Being pregnant and working was not difficult for me. I received some good advice from Joan Jansen, another Physical Education teacher in Marshfield; she told me not to "baby" myself during my nine months of pregnancy. It made sense to me, so I had been teaching that Friday when Valerie was born.

In the Milz family, there was a wedding coming up on December 9th for Ray's sister Bev, who had been in our wedding and I didn't know what kind of dress to purchase to attend; big or little. On the 8th, Joan Jansen came into the pool area where I was teaching a swimming class. She had a maternity dress to lend me which I was going to have to shorten that night. That dress was never worn by me because I headed to the hospital that night. When I got home after my day of teaching, I explained to Raymond that I thought I needed to go to the hospital. In the three years we lived in Arpin, he always went to the barn every night for chores at exactly 5:30 pm. It was his schedule, and he would not deviate from that schedule. Because that hour was fast approaching for him to head to the barn; I called a neighbor, Sally Hartman to take me to the hospital. Sally's husband was our friendly personal banker who we had met a year earlier when we had our first and only overdraft at the bank. We had become good friends after his first visit to our farm. They lived in a new home about two miles from us. I was comfortable with the idea of going to the hospital with Sally because I felt Raymond would still have plenty of time to arrive at the hospital after he was done milking. I had been told that because this was my first baby, the labor could take longer. Let it be said, Raymond was not interested in going into the labor room with me, when I asked him about it, I received a definitive, "no." So off Sally and I went to Marshfield while Raymond and Glenn went to the barn to do the evening milking. Now there is the true definition of a full-service banker. Just before Marshfield, Sally saw a vehicle stranded by the side of the road. She asked me if I thought she should stop to help. "If you can deliver this baby," was my reply. I was thinking it wasn't going to take long to deliver when we reached our destination. It was decided we wouldn't stop which was a good idea because we arrived at the hospital about an hour before Valerie was born. Raymond and Glenn arrived about fifteen minutes after she did. When I called my parents to let them know about Valerie's arrival, Mom didn't believe me at first because of all the noise in my room. I was making the phone calls while those other three were enjoying a visit.

Now back to that dress I was going to wear to the Milz wedding. It didn't get shortened and was donated because Joan didn't want it back. On their wedding day, the bride and groom; Bev and Steve came to the hospital to visit me after the ceremony. The reason I couldn't go was easily understood, and if I remember correctly Bev, had promised me she would stop at the hospital if I had the baby. It has to be said that they were my best-dressed visitors in their wedding finery.

Because I had the option to keep Valerie in my room people that came to visit got to see her. It was an innovative program that the hospital was trying and we even had our picture in the Marshfield News Herald because it was new. My nurse explained that mothers with other children at home felt they needed their rest and didn't care for the opportunity. With the birth of your first child, when the baby sleeps, you can sleep, that doesn't happen with the second one.

It has to be recorded that Raymond did attend the Milz wedding I ended up missing. I don't recall when he told me about the experience, but I do thank the Lord from time to time that my husband is still with me. Apparently, he had his share of celebrating both the birth of his first child and his sister's wedding because, as he explained it in his own words, "I followed the center line home." The laws in our state are now much stricter than in the early 1970's; which was a good thing. When he did arrive home, he forgot to set the alarm. The next morning when he woke up, he realized he would need help if he were to get to Sunday Mass on time. He made a call to his "full-service banker" and got the help he needed to deal with the cows and complete his Sunday obligation. Glenn must have enjoyed helping Raymond because it wasn't long after that and Glenn was farming giving up his banking career.

A few of my high school students heard that I had Valerie, so they visited me in the hospital that weekend. It was after I didn't return to school on Monday that my students started to show up in small groups. At one point my nurse asked if they were wearing me out and if I was getting tired of all the visitors. No way; I enjoyed the attention and having Valerie had been just a little extra exercise for me. Back in those days we didn't have the baby and leave the hospital within twenty-four hours. I stayed until Tuesday because our furnace had to be replaced and my doctor allowed me to stay an extra day because he felt I would be more comfortable than going to a motel. Things have changed in a big way since the 70's because that would not happen today.

It was planned that I would go back to school after the Christmas break but after talking to my principal, Russ Knapp it was decided I could take off another week. My babysitter was going to be Sally Hartman which meant I only had to take Valerie for a short ride and I continued on to school. Sally had two boys, and she was excited about taking care of my daughter. She insisted that Val be in a dress every day when she arrived at the Hartman's home. Valerie had lots of pretty pink dresses because my students had given me many of them for her birth, so that was an easy request to complete. One of the things I was most concerned about was getting enough sleep and being ready to get to work in the morning. Valerie was getting up at least once a night, and I didn't find it easy to fall back to sleep. When she would get up, I never turned a light on and talked to her much. I just went about the task of getting her a dry diaper and something to eat all with the idea of getting back to sleep. I didn't need to worry about it because the first time she slept through the night was the first night before I headed back to school. She must have gotten the message that Mom needed her sleep because she almost never got up during the night once I was back to school.

Before Valerie was born, I would help Raymond in the morning and evening with chores. I never milked, but I helped put in cows and fed the calves. After Val had arrived, I didn't feel I could help in the morning because I would never leave her in the house alone and I didn't think I would have time to bath her and take one myself to get ready for school. Raymond had to do it all by himself in the morning which he was able to do. In the morning I would dress before I got Val up to get her fed and dressed. One morning I decided to clip her fingernails which was not my brightest idea. I cut one too close, and she started to cry. As I picked her up to hug and comfort her she wet down the front of me. Lesson learned, always put a diaper on a baby before cutting fingernails or hugging. Now I had to dress her and change my clothes, but we made it on time.

Sally and I took some time to shop in Marshfield a few months after Valerie was born. It didn't take us long to realize I knew lots of kids at the high school because it seemed like any place we went we were stopped by a student of mine to see my new baby. It didn't take Sally long to determine that the next time we went shopping together, we were going to Stevens Point or Wisconsin Rapids. I know how celebrities feel, but I did enjoy the attention and the chance to show off my baby.

It was the end of May 1973 when I realized just how good it was that Valerie didn't ride with me all the way to Marshfield. I had dropped her off at Sally's and headed to school which was going to be an easy day for me because it was a rainy day. It was a Friday, and the gymnasium where I taught was set up for graduation that weekend which meant my classes couldn't be held inside because of all the chairs and staging or outside because of the rain. I explain this, so others understand I was not speeding when I hit another car. In my defense, the car I hit was backing up to see how another driver was doing because the second vehicle was in the ditch. I saw the first car and knew it was moving slower than I was and that second one in the ditch caught my attention. When my gaze returned to the first car, I soon realized not only was I moving faster than she was but that she had come to a full stop on the road. It was not a good situation. Is it any wonder that I hit the gal? But after all was said and done; Valerie was not with me, and I had my seatbelt buckled. The car that I totaled that day was Ray's 1969 Ford Mustang. It was the first brand new car he ever purchased, and he knew it was the only new car being driven in Loyal for a few days in 1969. "Sorry about that Raymond," was all I could say.

Just as a note of advice, never put a child in a vehicle without a car seat and read the directions for the car seat you are using. The bottom line is that I don't think the car seat I had been using for Valerie would have been the best for that accident. When the dust settled, and I was able to head to Hartman's to pick up Valerie; by the time I arrived at Sally's I was in shock. What happened was both Valerie and I stayed at Hartman's because I needed to sleep for a few hours. Before I took my daughter anyplace after that accident, I had a new car seat where she faced backward when buckled in place. In 1972 I was not told that the seat needed to be in the back like it is in today's world. It is a wonder our kids are still alive.

One of my main concerns about being a "working mother" was that I might not see my daughter's first step. More than one person told me they did not want to work outside the home because they might miss something like those first steps. The one thing I have learned is that there is no end of ways to feel guilty about working and taking your child to a babysitter. But I got through all that and moved on to other things to be concerned about in my life. But back to Valerie's first step; I was thrilled the first time she stood up in the middle of the floor without assistance. I saw her doing it out of the corner of my eye. I called her to walk to me, knowing then I was going to see her first steps. She immediately got down on the floor and crawled to me. It took some patience on my part and convincing on Val's part but it was just a matter of days, and I saw her take her first steps.

During the Christmas season of 1973, there was an interesting event. Valerie was in the living room while I was in the kitchen getting supper ready. I heard a bang that made my heart stop. When I got to the living room, she was sitting at the top of the fallen Christmas tree. How that tree fell without landing on her is anybody's guess. I do believe she has a guardian angel and that just might be the only way to explain what happened in the living room while mom was not watching her.

Ray and I went to Milwaukee with Valerie to visit a friend of Ray's from high school, Don Bowe. His wife Barb and I went shopping at a large mall in the area. I didn't have any money with me, so Ray gave me twenty dollars. Barb remarked that those twenty bucks weren't going to take us far, but then I didn't need anything. While we were shopping, I had Valerie in a cart, and she was so good just looking around while I was checking on merchandise. At one point she wanted to get down, and I let her out just for her to walk around. As I turned to check out displays and looked back, she was gone. Talk about a sick feeling; I kept looking for her and coming back to my cart, then I went the other way and came back to where I started. Finally, I realized when I stopped to think that the little girl wasn't coming back to the cart so I ran to the front of the store to ask for help. The first thing they asked was, "what is she wearing?" It took a while for me to remember she was in red, white, and blue. What was going through my head was the question, what I was going to tell her father if I had to go back to Don and Barb's without her? The manager announced that there was a "lost mother" at the service desk which didn't make me laugh but when they explained what my daughter was wearing a man in the back of the store spotted her and told the woman next to him that he thought that was the child they were looking for. The woman took her by the hand and led her to the front of the store. That was a large store, and Valerie must have gotten out of the cart and just started walking. Again, all was good and turned out for the best.

Because we had signed a three-year lease on the farm in Arpin, we knew we wanted to purchase a farm of our own in the future. I enjoyed all our neighbors in the Arpin area, and I was not looking forward to leaving. After Valerie was born, I remember thinking now I could move any place because I had my little girl. We had been looking at lots of places. We did finally settle on one that was in the Vesper area but we were going to wait until the realtor was no longer eligible for a percentage of the sale. Then one night Arnie came over to tell Raymond about a farm he heard about in the Milladore area. I was invited to go with, but I had to get Valerie ready for bed, and I needed to prepare for the next day at school. There are lesson plans which are important to controlling a class. It was easier to maintain control of a class when you knew what you were doing and kept them moving. Thus Raymond and Arnie went to check out the farm in Milladore without me. It was getting late that evening when they got home and for a good reason. Raymond had put an offer in on a place that I had not seen. The papers he signed were contingent on the fact that he still needed to get financing. When he got home he explained that if I didn't like it, we could just say that the financing didn't happen, in other words, no bank would give us money. He went on to tell me about the place and as he talked I knew he was excited about that farm. He explained that the barn was the newer, rounded roof type, but the house isn't much. There are two silos in good shape, but the house isn't much. There is a conveyor system across the top of the barn to make it easier to get hay and straw in the barn, but the house isn't much. I was dubious about that place in Milladore, and I just had to ask if the house had running water? When he hesitated with his answer, I knew we had to look at this place again. He figured we could build a new house in five years once we settled on the place. The next day when I checked out the house which had a good furnace, running water, and a phone I knew we would build in less than five years because he was right, the house wasn't much.

The day I saw the place it was cloudy, overcast, and gloomy; actually, it was like that for at least a week after we had purchased the place. Once Ray picked up all the junk around the buildings and tore down some of the smaller buildings the place started to look pretty good. Raymond had a vision that was lost on me, but once he built the new pole shed and added an extension on the barn, it did start to take shape.

What we had ahead of us was lots of work if we were going to make the move to live in Milladore. We know that hard work is a reward in itself and with the right attitude can even make the work fun. Keeping all of this in mind, and knowing that fun is good, we decided to make our home in Milladore, Wisconsin.

CHAPTER THREE

"We don't meet people by accident; they cross our path for a reason."
Unknown

It was March of 1973 when we purchased the farm in Milladore. The night Raymond was bidding on the farm he was in the barn, and there was someone else in the house also interested in buying the place. That was the night before the auction which was when the machinery, cattle, and farm would be sold the next day. We found out that the man in the house wanted three cows for the same price Ray was willing to pay for the farm. Ray could have waited for the next day to bid at the auction, but he decided he wanted to seal the deal that night. The next day when people heard that the farm was no longer for sale, he felt some individuals were disappointed because they were interested in purchasing the place. He might have had to throw in a higher bid if he had waited. It was only recently that I think I figured out who was in the house bidding against Ray. Check the last chapter for that possible answer.

We owned the farm in Milladore for a year before we relocated to that place. I worked in the house to get it fixed up that first summer after we purchased the place. The water heater didn't work so when I went to the farm to clean in the house; I took an ice cream pail full of hot water with me as well as Valerie. She was only crawling at the time, but I had a playpen to keep her in one place. There was one time that I must have felt she needed to move around more than in that little space the playpen offered because I let her out. I was painting the woodwork with dark brown paint. I don't care for painted wood, but there was a lot in that old house that needed to be covered. What was I thinking? This is a question that crosses my mind now because she got both of her arms into that paint. When I picked her up, I wrapped both of her arms in a blanket to make sure she didn't put her hands into her mouth. Millie was our savior because she was able to help me get Valerie cleaned up. In those days I never went anyplace without a change of clothes for Val. Millie and Rudy Younger lived on the farm across the highway from us, and they proved to be fantastic neighbors.

When I was working on the house, I took all the old rugs and floor coverings off the living room and dining room floors to find a hardwood floor that had beautiful boards. I rented a floor sander to take the old paint and varnish off. Once I put on a new layer of stain and varnish on those floors were beautiful. The only issue was that the large circular sander didn't get into the corners because it was too big. I was told I could strip that portion by hand, but I just knew I wasn't living in this house on a permanent basis. My skills; or should I say lack of skills as a carpenter, were evident when I paneled the kitchen. When I showed Ray my hard work at the end of one day, he asked, "Why didn't you wait for me." There is a simple answer, he was a farmer, and I would still be waiting today.

Before we moved to our new farm, Nancy and David Wucherphennig, Ray's sister and her husband lived on our farm for about nine months to take care of the animals that we had in the barn so it would not freeze during the winter. David even did some field work for Raymond while they were living there. Raymond can remember that Dave was using our 190XT Allis Chalmers and got it stuck, at least it wasn't me. Once when Dave was plowing for Raymond, he found a PTO (power take-off) guard for a spreader that was in the field which he dragged out and put along the fence line. When the former owners of our place were trying to sue a businessman for selling them a manure spreader without a PTO guard, the businessman was extremely pleased to hear that David had found that guard. David went to court to testify that the guard was still on the fence line where he had placed it. The lawsuit didn't go well for the former owner of our farm. There were many rumors about those owners, and this was the only one we were involved in so it is the only one I'll record for posterity. Nancy and Dave had their daughter Sheila who went to Kennedy school for kindergarten that year. It was the school my two children attended years later, and we'll get to that in chapter six.

There was a plan to get all our machinery moved to our new location. Raymond had it figured that he would put crops in on the farm we were renting in Arpin and then move each piece of machinery as he needed it in Milladore. In theory, it was a good idea but add reality, and it doesn't work as planned. It was the weather that was an issue. One field in Arpin would be ready then a field in Milladore, then another field in Arpin, so the machinery went back a forth a few times. Because I was in school during the spring planting it wasn't always my responsibility to move the machinery. We had built two sheds to store the machinery. Menards was having a sale on sheds, so we put up a 40 X 63 and a 40 X 45. Ray also wanted an extension on the barn to cover the barn cleaner, so a third Menard shed was built, but at the time he wanted it to be the same width as the barn, so he had to pay extra for the 36 X 45 addition because it wasn't the standard size that was on sale. Because hindsight is 20/20, he decided he should have put up the standard larger size because the extra few feet could have been toward the back and the front of the barn would have looked even.

One of the first times we baled in Milladore we had some Timothy hay to bale. Because we still had some hay that would be moved from Arpin that field of Timothy was offered for sale. Ray said the people that purchased it also helped bale it and it was sold for 10 cents a bale. Because they didn't take all of it, we had extra bales which he put in our barn on the bottom of the hayloft as insulation. That was excellent insulation for many years and also proved to be expensive insulation. In 2012 when Raymond decided he could sell that layer, he sold it for $4.00 per bale. To say prices have changed dramatically since 1973 would be an understatement.

When we made the move to Milladore, Rudy and Millie Younger were not the only people we knew. Those ten cows Ray had purchased a few years earlier from John Hollar were coming back to Milladore. Hollars now were going to live one mile from us. This would be the reason I can remember where at least ten of our first cows had been purchased. Hollar's oldest daughter was Valerie's first babysitter.

Millie enjoyed Valerie and wanted her to call her "Grandma." I figured it would not offend any the real Grandparents, so we were fine with the idea. Once when we saw her in Marshfield while I was shopping, it wasn't ten minutes later that Millie was back with a doll for Valerie because, that is what Grandmothers do, spoil kids.

Loretta Mancl, the owner of Mancl's grocery store in Milladore, told me she was so pleased to realize that we were Catholic after she had seen us in Church on the first Sunday we worshiped at St. Wenceslaus. I questioned her about what she meant, and she explained there were four Catholic churches within 10 miles of our farm, so it was just easier if we were Catholic. Being Catholic has been a long tradition in both mine and Ray's family. When we did join the church, I told Father Donald Berg, the parish priest at the time that I was excited to live within walking distance of the church. He said, "You never will walk." He was right, but I did cross country ski once to a Christmas Eve Mass because of a snowstorm. I had guests coming the next day; I knew if the snow was cleared and my guests could come, I didn't have time to go to church on Christmas day. I stored my skis in a closet when I got to church that was taken out when the church was remodeled. It was Father Berg who gave me a church directory from 1972 to use to learn the names of people in the area.

Once we moved into our new home, many of the "issues" had been solved. Let me explain. Remember that Nancy and Dave had lived there for nine months before we moved. We had replaced the water heater, but it did seem like she would call us often to explain what the latest issue was that we needed to correct. I know there was a problem with the furnace and the well. At one point they were out of water, and we found we needed a new well. It was just those ordinary things that all landlords have to do.

When a person lives on a farm, there is an assumption that you will have a garden. My garden didn't work out very good in Arpin because it was next to Ray's cornfield one year and when he sprayed the corn for weeds, he thought he would help me out in the garden and sprayed it. As my little plants started turning brown, he realized that "help" was not such a good idea. At our new place, I claimed some land across the driveway as a garden. If you talk to Ron Hartman, he will bring up the fact that I did plant cucumbers to pick for a pickle company. It never was a good idea because it was a lot of work and I didn't have the time. I grew more weeds than cucumbers. Through the years the garden has been moved closer to the milk house because it makes it easier to water. Besides vegetables, in the garden, I liked to plant flowers. I read that rabbits do not like marigolds, so I outline my garden with them; they are so easy to grow a person would think they are weeds if they didn't look so good. There is an odor that is noticeable that does keep the little varmints away from the vegetable plants.

Another thing I liked was to plant flowers by old wagon wheels. When I was driving past Alfonse Benish's place on the county line road, I noticed an old wagon with four wheels in one of his fields. I stopped to ask how much he wanted for that wagon. The price was right, so I ended up with four wagon wheels to plant flowers around. He also offered me an old wooden skidder that he had used to pull logs out of the woods. The two pieces of wood on the sides curved up and he explained it took his father a long time to find just the right curve on both logs. I tipped it up against our garage and put a hanging flower basket on it. While we were visiting, Alfonse told me that the large wooden cross at the front of our church was also made by his father, Stephen Benish.

When I would get to school in the morning, I would take off ASAP for a run. In those days I would do two or three miles which got me around the neighborhood by the high school in Marshfield. Once when returning as I was running up the driveway, there was a car coming in; because it could have been a teen driver, I moved onto the grass so there would not be an accident. Back in those days, I wasn't worried a kid would run you down, just because someone is bullying them and teachers aren't helping them cope. That "bully issue" is another story, so I'll come back to it. The car was green, no I don't know what the make or model was because all I saw was green. It pulled into the parking lot and stopped, which allowed me time to catch up and run by it. As I passed the car, I glanced at it to see who it was arriving at school. It was a guy with his pants down to his knees; yes, all was exposed. It has been said you should never react to an exhibitionist, so I calmly jogged on. As I got closer to the door of my locker room, I realized "I am the adult here" as well as "I am the teacher here." I have to identify this guy and report this to the main office. I turned to look, and the green car was off in the distance driving out of the parking lot. Next, I called my vice-principal, Bob Leu, and he asked me to report to the office; didn't care for the sound of that but I knew it was necessary. When I got to his office, he was on the phone but waved me in to have a seat. I could tell by listening to one side of the conversation, he was on the phone with the police and they were talking about my little situation. As he hung up, he explained we were going to the police station so I could look at mug shots. I tried to explain to Mr. Leu; I had not seen his face. If he walked into Bob's office, I would not have known if it was him unless he still had on plaid pants with a brown or tan hue. Mr. Leu didn't laugh at me; he was trying to be very professional when he said I had to go to the police station. When I was looking at the mug shots, the detective was trying to explain that I just might have seen the guy's face. I tried to assure him; I did not. My eyes did not wander to the man's face is all I have to say about this event.

When I would run at home, I had an excellent two-mile, four-mile or six-mile square to use with all of them starting and ending at the farm. It wasn't necessary to carry a stopwatch; I just placed my watch in the mailbox, checked the time as I took off and checked the time when I returned. If I was able to keep the time close to a 20-minute mile, I was happy. Those days and times are things of the past. I can tell you how I knew I lived in a small friendly town. The locals stop and ask if you need a ride. Once Hal Richardson stopped, and asked me if he could give me a ride home. He hauled our milk to Dairy State Cheese in Rudolph. I explained that I was out exercising and would get to my farm about the time he was finished picking up our milk. Another time when I saw Hal, he asked; "Now you do that for exercise, and you want me to drive by you?" I assured him I would be just fine.

During our first Christmas in our new home, Valerie received a rocking rider bouncy horse with springs from Santa. Too bad Santa didn't have it put together before he gave it to her; Raymond spent a full evening after milking putting the horse together. She enjoyed that horse, and it would move along the floor because the center of the living room was bowed, or lower. As she jumped, the horse would move toward the center of the room, and I just had to bring it back to the outside to start again. This was a great exercise for everybody.

The old house had three bedrooms, one on the lower level with the other two on the second level. We all stayed upstairs because we would never have heard Valerie during the night if she cried. Our farm was located about 100 feet from the railroad tracks. It was amazing how soon we were able to adapt to having trains pass by our place without hearing them. When people come to visit they usually asked how many trains pass our farm in a day. We never counted and if we were in the house most likely didn't hear them. I never allowed Valerie to play outside without me because of the train tracks being so close. Once when we were outside on the swing set, I realized I was dressed too warm for the day. I let her continue playing outside, and I ran upstairs to change into shorts. Before I even took my slacks off, I went to the window to see what was happening. Valerie was headed toward the tracks following her puppy. I moved fast to get to her before they reached the tracks. She came inside with me to change my slacks, and as we got back upstairs, I heard a train blowing its whistle off in the distance. That was close and sad to say that puppy never learned to stay off the tracks and was killed a few months later.

The stairs going to the second floor were steep and narrow. I painted them a gray and covered them in the middle with carpet. That carpet didn't make it any easier to go up and down which I found out the hard way. One Sunday afternoon when Valerie and I got up from a nap I was carrying her downstairs. I had nylons on, and my feet slipped out from under me. As I bumped down the rest of the way on my derriere, I held tight to Valerie and didn't put my hands back to break my fall. The trip down really scared her, and when we reached the bottom, she was crying. I just sat there on the floor, stunned by the trip down. Raymond came to check on us and took Valerie out of my arms to comfort her as he walked her around the house. Once her crying started to subside, he decided to check on me. "Are you OK?" he asked when he found me in the same place he had left me. Nothing was broken, and now years later I don't feel any aches or pains related to that eventful trip down those steep stairs. The carpet was not a good idea.

During one of our first summers in Milladore, we went swimming at Hefko pool in Marshfield. My sister Patricia was visiting from Michigan, and we thought it would be a great place to take our kids. I had only Valerie and Pat only had Lisa; two adults and two kids. We were going to the baby pool which was about twelve to eighteen inches at the deepest end. Raymond expressed concern about taking Valerie to the pool. It has to be said he is a non-swimmer and he didn't want her to drown. One more thing that has to be explained; I was the head swim coach at the high school in Marshfield for the girls' team. He was OK with me having twenty to thirty girls that I was responsible for but not his daughter.

That coaching job was gratifying, and if it had not been so time-consuming, I might have coached more than the fifteen years I did. When I was working during the day, I made a lot more money for my time teaching Physical Education than when I coached after school. But I found I did some of my best teaching after school because the girls I coached wanted to be on the team and wanted to do their best for the team. The only thing I didn't care for was the bus ride; it could get late especially if we had a swim meet in Rhinelander. Once after one of my longer trips, I arrived home, and Ray greeted me with a big smile and a warm washcloth. He and I had an agreement that he would clean the barn, and I would change the diapers. That night he was glad to see me because Valerie needed to be changed and he had made her wait as long as he felt he could. Welcome home.

Another time I didn't get home just when it was planned was during the summer I taught Drivers' Education. Gary Koehler was the department chair, and I told him I would teach two to four hours on any given day, but not an eight hour day like most of the instructors did. I liked my days short and sweet. The students in these classes were some of the most motivated individuals because once they were finished with the class, they only had a driving test to pass, and Wisconsin considered them ready to drive. I was scheduled for two hours but ended up teaching for four on several occasions. Once I knew Ray had field work for me, but I thought I had time before I was needed on the tractor. Because the hay was ready earlier and there was a promise of rain, Ray asked Millie Younger if she would drive a tractor for him. It was a bigger tractor than Millie had ever driven before but she told him, "If Connie Milz can do it, I can too." It never happened because I arrived home just before they were ready to start; I think Millie was disappointed she didn't get to give that tractor a try. I am sure she would have enjoyed the experience.

It is hard to remember when we first met all of our friends Milladore. The area was, and still is, populated by friendly rural people that were willing to help us even if we did not ask. I want to write about all our friends, but every time I review this chapter I come up with someone I forgot. If you are reading this and find I missed you, please don't hate me just think about Alzheimer's. Granted I have not been diagnosed, but how could I forget you?

Bill and Annette Fuehrer have five children; Cheryl was the oldest, and she was followed by four boys. Annette was an excellent baker and cook which should have been an inspiration to me, but it wasn't. No one ever died from eating with us, and my kitchen came with the house, or I could have done without one. Their family belonged to our church and Bill worked at the local Ford garage; someplace between the church and the garage is where we met.

Vicki and Keith Trowbridge also belonged to our church, and I know I met Vicki at one of the women's church meetings when I worked one of the church dinners. I do remember playing bingo with her after meetings, and some of the more serious players were not happy with us because we did more visiting than playing. We seldom won, but there is no reason to wonder why.

Another family was Ed Stashek's that we met while attending church. "Now you are going to join a good parish," was the comment from Judy, Ed's wife. I had just learned that Father George Stashek, our parish priest from Arpin was her brother-in-law. He was standing next to me when she made the comment. When I reacted with surprise, he explained that it was OK because St. Wenceslaus was his home parish.

Heading east on what was Highway 10, toward Milladore, our neighbors were the Tony Peterson family. He also worked at the garage in town when we first moved to Milladore. He and his wife Hazel had a few children that were already grown and out of the house; those that were still at home were older than my Valerie. If you head north out of our driveway on County Road S, there is the John Hollar family. In chapter five I write more about that family with their ten children.

On May 24, 1975, Francis Cherney wrote us a letter. He and his wife Beverly live one mile from us on the farm that Francis has called home for his entire life. He wrote us as the President of District 12B of Associated Milk Producers, Inc. We had been asked to represent 12B in the 1975 Outstanding Young Dairy Couples contest. Note the contest was for farming couples and so at the state level, we didn't win. The winners that year were Mr. and Mrs. Ojars Rekis from Marshfield. They farmed 655 acres, had 165 animals, and had the highest butterfat production in Wood County. One of the judges explained to us that he felt our way of farming might be the new wave. He was talking about the fact that I worked out of the home for a salary and health insurance while Raymond ran the farm. I did my part for the good of the farm, but it didn't help us with this contest. I mention all of the above because of the P.S. Francis added to his letter. I quote, "May I also add that it is a pleasure to have you folks as neighbors. You've made your place pleasing to the eye, and your being here is a definite asset to the community. We hope you like it here, too."

We were so fortunate to have some good friends and acquaintances at our new location. Because we enjoyed our neighbors from when we lived in Arpin I was concerned about moving to a new place. Today many of the people we met in both Arpin and Milladore are looking down at us from heaven. If you look at the stars in the night sky it has been said that they might not be stars but holes in heaven that lets the love of our friends and relatives shine down on us. What do you think?

After living in our first home in Milladore for about three years, we were ready to build a new home. Raymond had said we could afford it after about five years, but I moved it up about two years. Part of that first home was the original log cabin because we could see the logs in the crawl space under that section. The floors in that space were so slanted toward the center that Valerie could stand in the middle of the floor in the living room and roll a ball toward a wall and it would come back to her. My mantra became, "No time like the present to build a new home."

CHAPTER FOUR

"You live, you learn, you upgrade."
Unknown

In the summer of 1976, we started building a new home, which was placed to the west of the old home. We were able to watch the new place go up from the comfort of our home until that September. There was a good furnace in our older home but, it was going to be too small for the needs of the new place. We sold the furnace out of the old home and purchased a new oil furnace which was installed. When we were building, Raymond said he would never burn wood in the new place. Once the new place was completed, he decided he had lots of wood and wanted to use it to heat the new home. After our home was finished, we put up an extra chimney because the one going up the middle of our place could not be used for wood heat. It was not nice seeing the guy cut into the side of our new roof for that wood chimney but over the years we have found some advantages to having two chimneys. We do enjoy the wood heat, and I never had to test the theory about wood warming a person more than once which means I never made the wood. Raymond is the one that tested the theory that wood will keep you warm while you are making it, throwing it in, and when it is burning in the furnace.

When we did decide to build, Erlin Young was teaching with me at the high school, and he built homes on the side. He had already built several homes for his family, and they would move into the new place and sell the old one. I asked him if his wife liked the idea of moving every two or three years. He explained the newer house was always bigger and better than the last one, so it made a move worth all of the hassle. For our new house, we were going to just work on the main floor, then work on the upstairs in a few years. But on the day Erlin was going to order all the woodwork for the house he asked if we wanted to order woodwork for the upstairs or cut it from the budget. Raymond said order it all; so with his OK in mind, we did just that. Over the years he has always paid all the bills and kept his budget in mind. If we had not ordered the woodwork for the upstairs, it might never have been completed. That may seem like a pessimistic attitude, but on a farm, a budget can get tight.

Erlin drew up some plans for me from my ideas of what I wanted; once on paper my house looked like a box. I knew what I wanted, but I didn't know how to build it. He asked me to explain what I needed which was two separate entrances. One entrance would be for Raymond to come into from the barn and another for visitors and guests to enter. I also needed a place for Raymond to be able to sit and eat during the day without changing out of his barn clothes. A guy can't change clothes every time he comes to the house because a dairy farmer is in and out all day. Erlin had lived on a farm and knew just what I needed. Once he drew up the second set of plans, I knew he had designed my new home. It was his idea to have two separate closets in the back entrance. We have a barn closet and a "not" the barn closet. When we came in from the barn for the night, barn clothes were hung in the barn closet. Other clothes in "not" the barn closet were snowmobiling suits but not the Sunday best or company's coats; there is a closet in the front hall for those items. I would never have thought of two closets and the fact that anything in that barn closet will take on the odor from the barn.

Instead of having our home with the front door facing the railroad tracks we designed it with the front door facing to the east. When people come in the driveway, they see the front door and come to that door. The service door Raymond uses to come in from the barn is on the side of the garage facing the barn, and people can't see it so they will use the front door. Erlin told me that if I leave the garage doors open, people will come in through the garage instead of going to the front door. He was right, most people will use the back door when my garage doors are open, so I keep them closed.

The last item on my list of options for our home was a place for Raymond to sit during the day in his barn clothes. We designed a bigger kitchen, and there was room for a reclining chair or sofa. Over the years we have had many different sofas or chairs but have found we like the double recliners the best. This option gives both of us a recliner, so there is no fighting, not that Raymond and I have done much fighting. We have very little to fight about, but that is one of those subjects that is open for debate.

There were three teachers from Marshfield that built my new house during the summer of 1974; those three usually found something like that when they were on summer break. They were Dick Johnson, Bernie Kraus, and Dennis Suckow; all of them worked in the tech department at the high school with Erlin. There was another man, Sid Reek; I had forgotten his last name, but Raymond remembered. Sid was a carpenter by trade, and he is the one that did the finishing work on the house after the others went back to teaching in September. This crew brought their lunch with them every day, but the last time they were going to be working on our home, we grilled out. It was a beautiful summer day and sat we outside at a picnic table to eat.

Once the basement was in for the new place, Erlin had me work on knocking off the steel rebars, which is short for reinforcing bars that were used to make the cement stronger. Those bars stuck out on the inside and outside of the walls. I was working on the outside when I was home alone, and a strong wind started to blow. I was next to the outside basement wall which means I was below ground level when I saw the wind blow one of the large doors off our shed. Now that was an experience I will never forget, and it gave me an idea of what it would be like to be in a tornado. I know I could never be a storm chaser; I don't even care to watch those shows on TV when I know I am safe in my home.

When Erlin and his crew started on the house, there was another day with strong winds. He asked me if I had the new house insured, which I did not because it wasn't up. He told me to get it insured now and insure it for the entire amount which at that time was around $35,000. His logic for doing it all at once was that as it got built, I would not have to keep calling my insurance company. He also explained that the materials were in my yard and they needed to be insured. Again, it is always a good idea to listen to the professionals.

There was a plan to move into the new home slowly, packing and then unpacking as I would take our things to the new place. Both homes were available to me, and there was no rush because no one was moving into the old farmhouse. Remember the part about selling the furnace; it was getting cold in the old home as summer changed to fall. Raymond told me about a cold front that was coming in, so we had to make a move over one weekend. I opened a window on the side of the old home and would pass boxes out to someone to take it in the front door of the new place. It was a smooth move that way, but the unpacking part took weeks, not the way I had it planned but a person has to go with the flow.

There were only two things that I did to help keep the cost of building the house down: first, on the hottest weekend of the summer we insulated the place. It wasn't planned that way, we didn't want to do it on the hottest weekend, but we were just unlucky. If we were going to do the insulating, it had to be done that weekend because the drywall was going up the following Monday. Ray's sister Nancy and her husband, Dave Wucherphennig helped us, and they can tell you about the heat that weekend. Nancy always has such a positive attitude which made the work enjoyable. Everyone should know a person they can call knowing that they will project positive energy. I have Nancy on Ray's side and my sister Patricia on my side, who are both always in a good mood looking at the positive of any situation. This is not to say that others on both sides are not positive; just that those two are dependable. As a disclaimer, these compliments are not made to detract from others. I do tend to surround myself with positive people.

The second thing, I did to keep costs down was staining of all the woodwork. Why? Because I was under the impression that is what people do. The issue I had was it took a long time for the staining to get done and the finish on the oak doors was not as good as it should have been if the task had been completed by a professional. Years later I took all the doors off and had them refinished by Wood Specialties in Milladore. Now when I dust them my cloth doesn't get caught on a rough surface.

What went wrong with these two projects? At one point we were having trouble heating the house, and the pipes in the upstairs bathroom were freezing when we got an east or west wind during the winter. The problem was solved when Tom Weinfurtner suggested that Ray insulate the soffits under the roof. This would have been done if I had left it to the professionals because once that was completed it was so much easier to heat our home and we never had a problem again with the pipes upstairs. With the second project, because it took me so long to complete the staining I wanted to know what I saved so I asked Sid how long it would have taken him to do the staining and finishing work. It would have taken him less than two days which doesn't seem like much of a cost savings to me. My thought is that life is an education especially if a person can learn from the mistakes they make. I learned a lot from building my home, one of which is I never want to build another one.

Once the new house was up, it was time to get rid of the old one. Allie Steppa from Milladore asked me what I wanted for the old place. I told him he could have it for nothing; which a friend of mine, Ken Flanagan, an art teacher from the high school said was not right. Ken felt I should have asked for enough money to fill in the hole once the house was moved. I didn't want any money from Allie because it was easier just to let him take it than for me to tear it down. So Allie moved it across one of our fields, down Otillia Lane and placed it on a basement near a barn that he owned. I have no idea what the cost of that move was, but I do know that no one ever lived in the place again. When Yogi Mancl purchased that farm, he and his wife Elaine tore it down and built a new home. My old place had outlived its usefulness, and it was for the best.

Millie Younger was always impressed with the way I had our new house built meaning the direction it was facing which was toward town. I didn't have to put the new one on the exact spot which was a great idea of Erlin's, and I am so glad I took the suggestion made by a professional. The only thing I wanted to do was build the house back further from the railroad tracks and add the two car garage after we took an old garage down. Now, more than 40 years later I realize the way we did it worked out just fine. I was concerned about a train derailment and the possibility of the house being hit. I was told the house was too far back even with the garage already in place to make that a concern. Just after we had built the house, there was a major derailment in Auburndale, and none of those cars would have touched my house if it had happened right in my front yard.

At one point I had my new house, but there was so much yet to be done. In the house, we had put flooring in the kitchen and entrances as well as the two bathrooms. The three bedrooms and the living room were just bare wood. Also, the lawn was not finished so I didn't have any grass which made for less mowing. I think we mowed around the mounds of dirt left from the construction for almost two years. I just kept telling myself at least I had the new home and everything would be completed in time. It amazes me when you see a place go up and be finished in days. You know that all the work was done by professional builders.

There was still some lawn around the new house that had been there from the old place which gave us enough room to have a swing set for Valerie. I didn't allow her outside on her own because of the train tracks, but I would work in the garden or mow while I was outside with her. Once when she wanted me to push her on the swing, I realized she was old enough to learn to "pump" to swing herself. I taught her in a few easy steps, except the last one. She was having a wonderful time in the summer sun swinging back and forth until she wanted to stop. By the time she got my attention, she was crying; "How do I stop?" "Just hold still and stop pumping," is what I told her. Such a short-sighted mother I could be at times.

In my defense, I was trying to take classes to complete my Master's degree. Once a person starts a program, they have to complete the degree within seven years. My first six credits that I had taken to move up on the pay scale I didn't even bother to try to use because I knew I would not be able to get twenty-four additional credits in less than fours years which I would still need for a degree. I started a Masters program at the University of Wisconsin-Stevens Point about the time we were building our new home. One funny event, I can laugh now, but not at the time; was when Valerie was in first grade we were both sitting together at the dining room table to work on our paperwork. Mine was a paper to submit for a class and Valerie was going through her kindergarten papers. We saved everything she brought home and put them in a box. She liked to go back and look at her work. I had plenty of time to work on my paper because the deadline was a month away. When it was time for me to submit my final paper, it was nowhere to be found. Note, my master's degree was earned by doing the work on a typewriter, so it was not saved on a hard drive. I had my rough draft, I had my notes, and I did have a weekend to write. There was no choice, so I wrote it again. I was disappointed in myself because I had completed the paper early and now I had to write under a lot of pressure. After that paper was graded, I found the first paper. The first one was in with Valerie's papers; we must have picked all her stuff up and slide mine in with hers. Once I looked over that first paper, I don't think it was as good as the second one that I was forced to write, which earned me an A.

Now with my new home in place, I had to remind myself that at some point in time everything would be completed. This does not mean that I didn't push to get it to where I would consider it complete. Ray told me that for Christmas of 1976 we could order the carpeting for the three bedrooms and the living room. Nice. I was off and running to the local carpet shop. I selected carpeting for the bedrooms which was the same for all three rooms. I was told if I did it that way it would save some money because there would be less wasted carpet. It took me longer to find what I wanted in the living room, but finally, I found a bright floral print with red roses. When I told Raymond about the cost, he checked our finances and explained we could do the bedrooms but there wasn't enough money to do the living room. While I didn't like the idea that I would have pictures of our first Christmas in our new house with the bare floor, I reminded myself that I had my new house and I would enjoy Christmas.

During this time, back in 1976, we were still using only one checking account. When it came time to file taxes, he was able to separate or find what he needed, so we kept our money together. The living room rug and Christmas of 1976 changed our minds. We needed to go to two checking accounts in the New Year. Why? Let me explain. The way I thought it out, because at one time we had enough money for four rooms of carpeting and now we had only enough for three, there would still be enough for a new pool table. It wasn't a new pool table; I found it in the paper. This was back in the day that you checked the local newspaper for classified ads instead of Craigslist. Because we were all upstairs in the new house and not using the main bedroom downstairs, I felt I had room for a pool table. When it was delivered it was a surprise for Raymond; the funny thing was that he had ordered the carpeting for the living room as a surprise for me. We had spent the same money, and the only thing that saved us was our savings account. But when you are on a farm, money in a savings account is earmarked for something other than spending too much money at Christmas time on presents. To make a long story short, we were both really surprised that Christmas.

Because I didn't know when the new carpeting was being installed, I already had the Christmas tree up, so Ray got Sally Hartman to help him clear out the living room before they came to install the carpeting in the room. He had scheduled it to be installed while I was at school; I think it was the last day before Christmas break that year. The only reason I looked in the living room that evening before Raymond came in from the barn for supper was because of a small antique barrel which was sitting in the kitchen. I used that barrel as an end table in the living room, and it didn't make sense that it was sitting in the kitchen. As I walked into the living room, I was so surprised because there was my carpeting. Sally had worked hard moving all the furniture and tree out for a few hours and then helped get the room back to the way it was. If Raymond had told me about the carpet, I could have waited with putting the tree up. Once Christmas was over that year we decided to divide our money into two checking accounts; one for the farm and one for daily needs. Our names were on both accounts but Raymond used only the farm account, and I used the other one.

In early spring of 1977, Bill and Annette Fuehrer were going on a vacation over a weekend. They had a small dog that stayed in their house, and they asked us to keep it for a day because their daughter Cheryl was busy and would pick the dog up late that evening. Annette knew I didn't want to let the dog in the house and she was OK with that idea. The dog did stay outside during the day when it was at their home. Valerie loved to play with the little puppy, so it was going to be a good deal for everyone. I just have always felt that on a farm our animals stay outside because we have a barn for them and people stay in our house. I know there are many people that disagree with me but we are all different. Back to Valerie's story and Annette's dog; they played together after lunch for about three hours. We had the dog on a leash, so the two of them stayed together, and every time I checked on them they were fine until Valerie decided to see what the mud in the back yard had to offer in the way of fun. Because the lawn was not finished, there were piles of dirt sitting around. This was so tempting to Valerie. When I went out the dog was sitting watching her but she was stuck in the mud and as I went to lift she came out of her boots. She was a mess, so the only thing to do was get her in the bath tub.

I drew a warm bath for her in the downstairs bathroom because it was time to get supper ready for Raymond. He liked to eat before the evening milking, and we always had to stay on schedule for those cows. After getting the dog in the cage Fuehrer's had left for us to use in the attached garage, I went in to check on Valerie. It wasn't just because of the mud that she needed a bath before supper, as I got close to her, she smelled like the dog. They had been playing so hard together she picked up an odor that had to be washed away. She was in the tub, flat on her back, sound asleep. The water didn't even come up to her ears, but the Lord was watching out for my daughter. I washed her up, took her out of the tub, and she didn't wake up. That afternoon outside with the dog had been very exhausting for the little girl.

It was time to get the lawn in place. Ray's big farm equipment could not be used. We had some neighbors that lived just past Peterson's that had just put in a new lawn. They used an old box spring to level their lawn. Using their old box spring and a small seeder Raymond was able to put in the lawn. After the grass was growing, it was time to put in a flower garden. On a farm, there was always plenty to do in the spring with planting and making hay. So when my Dad offered to help Raymond during the spring of 1977, it seemed like a good idea to say yes to any help that we could get. It was even a better idea for me because I wanted to put in that flower garden where we had taken trees out when putting up the new house. So as my Dad and I were working on that project, planting flowers he mentioned that when he called, he was thinking of something more like a "tractor job." It never occurred to me that he would rather help Raymond instead of me. Since those days my Dad helped on my sister's Pam's farm but then they always had a tractor job for him, and her boys made sure Grandpa could get up on those bigger tractors.

During all this building, getting the lawn in, and making my home livable; Dad told me that Grandma Eder, my maternal grandmother would like to take me downtown to show me off. Mom and Dad had been visiting Grandma in Earlville, Illinois where she lived. He explained that I should take some time to visit her and let her meet Valerie. We made plans for a visit to Illinois. After we returned from our visit, I asked Dad if he realized that Grandma would shift to reverse without putting her foot on the brake. "You didn't let her drive, did you?" was his question. I explained he had not told me not to let her drive only that she wanted me to go to town for coffee and show us off to her friends. This situation would be what a person could call a lack of communication.

It was nice that we were able to build a new house while the kids were still living at home; actually, it was built before Kevin was born. There was lots of activity in our lives then; I got a new car, a new house, and a new baby all within 18 months. The car was purchased from Hughes in Milladore which I believe was the first one of many vehicles we purchased from them. Dealing with them has always been good. I especially like getting my oil changed I just call them and leave the car home that day. When you get home from work, the car has been picked up, oil changed, and returned to my garage. They don't park it as I do so I can always tell if it has been moved as well as the bill is on the front seat; a dead give-a-way that we are ready to hit the road new engine-oil.

CHAPTER FIVE

"Don't dream it, be it."
Unknown

Once we had our new house built, we decided it was time to have a second child, maybe a boy. That is what they call an American family, a boy and a girl, not necessarily in that order. The due date for this baby was July 11, 1977, allowing me five weeks before going back to school. When I arrived at the hospital to give birth, I was the seventh woman there in labor, because there were only six labor rooms I was in the hall when my doctor saw me. He said, "She has to be in a room." This was because Dr. Stevens knew me and remembered that it didn't take me long to deliver Valerie. I was put in a room, not sure who had to give one up, but my nurse said I was the first one to have a baby on the floor that day. Just as a side note, Kevin was bigger than Valerie, so it did take me two hours of labor with him.

Kevin Ray was finally born on July 22nd, giving me only four weeks before the start of school that September. It was all just fine because I was able to get

Vicki Trowbridge, a good friend from our church who would watch both of the kids. She was the only person that had them both because the next year I wanted Valerie to go to a pre-kindergarten type class, and I felt Kevin was too young to go to that type of setting.

Naming Kevin was an interesting story; he was going to be Chad Edward until he was born. While I was in the hospital, Raymond asked me if I thought he, meaning our new baby, would like that name. It was obvious that Raymond did not, even though Edward had been his father's name. I had two names selected before the baby was born; Chad Edward for a boy and Kimberly Lynn for a girl. I had been thinking about Stephanie Lynn for a girl but my sister Pat had taken both the first and middle name for her second child, so I changed to Kimberly Lynn. Pat and I were both expecting in 1977, and she had her third girl three months before Kevin. She took my girl's name, so I had to have a boy. The name, Lynn was coming from Valerie's middle name. I just felt it would be neat if both my girls had the same middle name; don't ask why I don't have a good reason. After I named Kevin; using his father's name, Ray for his middle name, Patricia and I were talking. She explained that the name she had selected if her third child had been a boy was Kevin John. John was going to be the middle name because John Sauber was her husband at the time. Just for the sake of review, Patricia has three girls, not an American family.

My sister Pam had a boy just a month before Kevin was born. She was the sister I visited in the hospital on my due date for Valerie back in 1972. She had two more girls after Jenny; they are Peggy and Jodi. Now she had her fourth child who was her first boy, Patrick. Ray and I are his God-parents. To complete Pam's family, she and Randy had three more boys; John, Kurt, and Kris.

When I took Kevin home and saw him next to my Valerie, I realized she wasn't a baby anymore. Wonder how long it would have taken me to decide she was growing up if I had not had another child. For baby gifts, he received two little green outfits that were the same but different sizes. One was for six months, from a group of my students, while the second was for 12 months from my sister, Pat. When he fit into the bigger outfit, I sent her a picture of him. She told me she was pleased that my "little runt" was growing. I didn't know what she was talking about; he was not a little runt. Then I looked back at pictures of him in the first green outfit, yes he was tiny. It is a shame, but we never got pictures of him from the hospital because they were lost. One of those services that they most likely no longer provide because of the quality of pictures a person can get from their cell phone.

In the new house, our bedrooms were upstairs because there were two on that floor and I wanted to be on the same level with my kids. At first, I had Kevin's bassinette in our room. When he got too big for the bassinette, his baby bed was located on the landing at the top of the steps. It didn't take us long to realize he was a very light sleeper and we had to be exceptionally quiet downstairs after he went to bed. Not that we were so noisy once the kids went to bed, but the sound from downstairs went straight up the stairwell. What we did was move Valerie to the landing and Kevin's crib was moved into her room. Valerie had the smaller of the two bedrooms upstairs so when Kevin was moved into that one it became his room. Years later when we moved to the main bedroom downstairs, Valerie went into the bigger room. If there were things like baby monitors back when my kids were born, I didn't know about them, and I wouldn't have had the money to spend on them. We just slept on the same floor as the kids. It has been said that you move a baby out a bassinette when he or she is hitting the sides of the bed. Valerie didn't have to be moved to a baby bed until she was two months old. My son was a different issue. He was a "creeper" meaning he moved forward in his sleep. When he was only six days old, the little guy creped right off the bed. I had just feed him, and when he fell asleep, I placed him in the middle of our regular size bed to go downstairs for breakfast. All of a sudden I heard this thud and told Ray it couldn't be Kevin. After that, we heard him screaming, and we knew it was Kevin. I went running upstairs to find him tangled in the bed sheets. When I picked him up, he was really agitated. Can you blame him?

Not long after that incident or mishap, Raymond asked Valerie if she had been able to hold her little brother. At that point, the answer was no; so after he had calmed down I sat her down on our bed let her hold him. He wasn't real impressed at first because I don't think she was holding him tight enough but it didn't take long, and she was able to hold him without him getting upset. It was not long, and they were best of friends, and she was very protective of her little brother. There is a picture of an angel standing guard over two small children as they are crossing a bridge. The little girl in the picture is a head taller than the little boy, and she is guiding him as they are walking together. On Amazon it is titled; Guardian Angel with Children on Bridge. I was explaining to my Father that this was my favorite "angel" picture and it is also his. When I told him I think of my children when I see that picture he laughed. This is because my son's personality is one of being a very independent individual. In the picture, the little girl is the older of the two children, and she has her arm around the smaller boy to guide him across the bridge. Valerie did look out for her younger brother when he was a little guy.

My first week back to school after Kevin was born went just fine until it came to Friday of that week. That night I drove to Trowbridge's to pick the kids up but when I got there found I could not drive home, which was about six miles. It was my first migraine headache that was my downfall. Vicki drove my car home while her husband, Keith followed in their car to take her back home. I think a neighbor girl; Cheryl Fuehrer came and watched the kids until I could deal with the nausea. All you have to do with a migraine is get sick and sleep it off. Would you believe my Uncle John and Aunt Diane were visiting when I arrived home? They had a baby gift for Kevin, and I was too sick to do much more than say thank you and go to bed.

Going to church on Sundays was never an issue for Valerie because I would save a few ounces of her morning bottle to give her when she got fussy in church. Kevin was a different story. To start with you could not feed him anything extra because he would throw it all up. When he was supposed to get four ounces, if you gave him five the burp cloth was the only thing that saved you from wearing his entire morning bottle. How did I know what the "magic" number was? Hit and miss was the method I had to use. Saving some of his morning bottle didn't work because once he had a few ounces and I quit feeding him, you could not give him more. What I had to do was leave him at the babysitters when we went to Mass. It didn't prove to be much of a problem because Cheryl Fuehrer, now her last name is Nigh, was right on the way and she would meet me at the door of her parent's home to take charge of little Kevin.

Cheryl was also my first cleaning lady. Teaching, cleaning house and having two kids was not working very well for me at first. On Saturday I wanted to clean house, but I needed someone to mind the kids. I didn't want to hire another babysitter to play with my kids while I cleaned my house; instead, I hired Cheryl to clean my house while I played with the kids. I don't remember if she helped me for three or fours hours on a Saturday morning but I know she did a great job and I enjoyed the time I was able to spend with my children.

There was also the issue of the Friday night fish fry. The Friday night fish fry is a tradition in Wisconsin, and that is a favorite of Raymond's. We had always enjoyed going out after milking for a fish fry until I had kids; I didn't like picking my kids up from one babysitter that had watched they during the day and take them to another to go out for a fish fry. Our new normal became ordering two fish fries "to go" and eating at home. Ray would eat one, and I could share the second one with the kids for a few years. At one point I was not getting enough to eat so, we had to order three. When that was no longer enough for the four of us, we just started taking the kids out to eat on Friday night.

The first September that I was taking the kids to different babysitters must have been the most difficult for me, but I don't remember it not being possible. I was younger then and I am sure that made a big difference, but don't refer to me as old because I will take offense. However, I do remember one morning that was eventful. Kevin liked oatmeal, and I would not let him feed himself on mornings when we were getting ready to leave for sitters and work. I would get the kids ready first and sit them down to breakfast while I got ready. I must have eaten on the run which I still do today. This particular morning I was feeding Kevin his oatmeal, but on weekends I would let him feed himself which means we had a big mess with plenty of time to clean it up. Kevin was always a very independent boy and had a mind of his own. On this occasion he decided he wanted to feed himself; because I was not getting any cooperation from him I decided he needed dry cereal to eat as finger food and I tossed the oatmeal. Keep in mind, Valerie was always protective of her little brother. Because he was crying that the oatmeal was gone she came over to me to explain; "He wanted that, I hate you." Well, now we were ready to start our day. After that, I dressed Valerie and let her eat but waited until Kevin was finished feeding himself. See a person just has to be adaptable and all will work out in the end.

When Kevin was just a baby himself, he wanted any other baby that was in the house on his lap. He enjoyed holding babies. After checking with Donna Milz about the ages of her kids, we do think it was Jennifer who was born in 1978 that had to be on Kevin's lap whenever they came to visit. Little Jennifer was not happy because Kevin wasn't much bigger than her and she wasn't being held as tightly as an adult would hold her. At issue was my son was quiet for a while when holding a baby but it never lasted very long, and he was ready to move again.

Once Valerie was in school, and Kevin was older I took him to Alliance Missionary church where Valerie had gone three years earlier. He learned a different Bible story that became his favorite; Daniel in the lion's den. As he would explain the story to you the way he said, "The Lord shut the lion's mouffs" was so cute. What can I say, my kids were just adorable. The year before he was going to start school I found a pre-kindergarten class at St. John's in Marshfield, the only problem was a babysitter. This would be the last time I needed one for my kids while I was teaching because Kevin would be in school the next year. On the first day, I took him to class and at noon when I went to pick him up, I asked the other mother's if they could recommend a babysitter. I either would find one or I was planning to take him back to school with me for the afternoon. That was during the week before classes started at the high school. Diane Reigel said she always did babysit but her daughter Becky was in this class and she didn't want to be tied down while Becky was in school. Because Kevin was in the same class, she decided taking him in the afternoon would work out fine and she still had some time to herself.

Because of the "school" setting at St John's when the teacher called me about my son's behavior in her class I told Raymond that I didn't think it would be the last call I would ever receive from a teacher if Kevin were in his or her class. At issue was that all of the twelve children in her class left one day without hugging her. She explained that my son was a leader in the class and he told all the other little kids that "hugs are icky" and they should not hug her. This was hard to believe because if you were to compare my two, Kevin would always hug and cuddle before Valerie would. The teacher felt that it might be because she was pregnant. I have no idea what was going on in his head, but what the teacher wanted me to do was explain to my son that he should not talk the other kids into not hugging her before they left the classroom but he didn't have to hug her. She was in the habit of dismissing each child by calling their name and giving them an opportunity to hug her. She planned to dismiss Kevin last. That morning at breakfast I talked to Kevin about hugs and who a person hugs, why to give hugs, and the fact that if he didn't want to hug his teacher, he didn't have to but don't tell the other little guys and gals what to do. Thus the stage was set, and the teacher called me that night to report how it went. She dismissed her class one-by-one, and everyone gave her a goodbye hug. Then with everyone out of the room, Kevin was dismissed and asked if he wanted to hug her. His reply was, "My mom said, 'I don't gotta' to do nothin' I don't want to do.'" I explained to the teacher that those were not my exact words, but he did get the gist of our conversation. At one of the teacher conferences, she explained that after it was no longer an issue, he even was hugging her when he left for the day.

Because John and Rita Hollar lived only a mile from us, I was always able to have a babysitter whenever we went out. There was a time that I got a babysitter while I was out in the field helping Raymond; keep in mind; I was his best tractor driver. He told me that once and I am sure that was after he tried to get others and found they were busy. Also, I was the driver that he didn't have to pay. Now that is a good deal for any farmer. The two oldest girls, Denise and Mary Lou, would never take money when they came to watch the kids if I was in the field. That was another very nice deal for us. As I went down the list of the Hollar children, I think Chris and Anna were the only ones that didn't babysit for us. Chris was born in 1971, just before Valerie, while Val and Anna share 1972 as their birth year. All ten of the Hollar children were born when we arrived in Milladore.

Because all but the youngest two babysat for me and took good care of my children, I feel I need to document their names with the year of their birth. Denise was born in 1961, Mary Lou in 1962, Mike in 1963, Carol (the Christmas baby) in 1965, Barb in 1967, Monica in 1968, Dawn in 1969, Pat in 1970, Chris and Anna are the youngest. Rita told me the way she keeps it straight is to remember Mike is the third oldest while her only other boy, Pat is the third youngest.

Once when there was a wedding in Milladore where all of the Hollar children that were old enough to babysit were going to be "employed" for the night, Rita called me to ask if we were going to need a babysitter that evening. We were not the only family that trusted our young children to the Hollar's. Rita explained she only had one babysitter left and there had been another call for a babysitter. Before she was going to let that last one go she checked with me and we did go to that wedding. Good neighbors like that are blessings.

There is one other babysitting story that I remember. Cindy Cherney was another neighborhood gal that watched my kids. One night she told me that she had not allowed Kevin to climb on the floor-to-ceiling lamp that we had in the living room. When she asked him to get down, he explained that his mom would allow him to climb on that lamp. Kevin could come up with some creative stories.

Before Kevin was in school the three of us would go swimming in the pool at Senior High while Raymond was doing the evening milking. As a teacher and swim coach there, I had a key which was nice because we could swim on our own timeline and not be concerned about the weather. I always liked to take another adult with me because what would happen to my kids if something happened to me? That lifeguard training drilled the idea into my head that you should never swim along and I just figured swimming with my two children when they were eight and four years old could be considered swimming alone. Marie Welch, the other Physical Education teacher, went with us a few times because she had two children of her own. I recall her saying once that she wasn't sure what she was going to do with her children one night because her husband was going to be gone. I told her I had plans to pick my two up and come back to the pool. The only thing she was concerned about was what she would feed them. My menu for the evening out was peanut butter sandwiches and apple slices. I would add a thermos of milk, and we had our meal. I am willing to bet the bread used to make the sandwiches was white and not wheat. We put the kids in life jackets and had a great time. A few times the neighbor girls, Cindy and Rhonda Cherney went with us. We usually just went to McDonald's when they were with us because it was just easier. The thing that I noticed was Cindy did not get dressed fast after swimming. I would be ready after dressing myself and my two kids, and we had to wait for her. Rhonda was faster, and also would be waiting for her older sister. Then when we got our food at McDonald's the first one done was Cindy. She is now a nutritionist; I wonder if she tells people to slow down when they eat so they can enjoy their food? That would be some good advice from a nutritionist.

Back to the issue of eating fast: I never wasted much time eating, but I was never as fast as Cindy. At other times when in Marshfield I would stop at McDonald's to feed the kids and then take something home for Raymond. I always made sure he was feed because I wanted him to keep his strength up to be able to milk those cows. It isn't safe to eat and drive, and if you let kids eat in a car, it can turn out to be a real mess. What we would do is order, and we sit inside to eat. Once as we sat down and had all our food in front of us Valerie started wrapping up her food and told Kevin to do the same. "Time to go," was her thought. I realized that when I had only Valerie, I would sit inside but not wait for her to finish. When I was done eating, and most of her meal was gone, I started wrapping hers up to let her eat in the car. One isn't as messy as two; must have been my theory. Now Valerie was doing the same thing to her younger brother. Slow down and relax for a few minutes became my mantra. I had to remind myself to enjoy the time I had with my kids.

Being a wife and mother has always been my favorite career choices. At times while I was teaching it was difficult to keep my priorities straight, but I knew I was a wife first, then a mother, and then a teacher. My husband worked hard at his job and tried not to complicate my life because he was a farmer. He job can't be defined by the clock; one just has to work until everything is done. I was always able to get excellent babysitters before my kids were in school and that made my ability to teacher easier. While the days were busy, I still found time to enjoy my children. Like the time we went downhill sledding in Wisconsin Rapids. Kevin must have been about two years old, so Valerie was six at the time. We found a hill that wasn't very steep which allowed you to slid down and walk back up. It was fun until Kevin decided he had to ride the sled up the hill which meant I did a bit of extra work. The last time he headed down he hit one of the tires which were placed on the sides of the hill to keep you from falling off the side of the hill. We could tell he was hurt because after that he would not walk. When we got home, he would crawl on the floor, and it appeared that when he did try to walk his leg was hurting him. If only that little guy could have told me what is wrong, it would have made my life easier. I took him into urgent care in Marshfield. When we were ushered into a room to see the doctor, I couldn't get him to settle down on the table. He was trying to climb and even walk by the time the doctor came to examine him. I explained to the doctor that he wasn't this good about two hours ago. That doctor assured me he understood but examined Kevin and found nothing wrong with him. If I would have just waited an hour or two but Kevin was old enough that he had not been crawling for more than a year. It is better to be safe than find out later something was broken.

Another thing that I enjoyed doing with my young children was "trick or treat." We would just stay in our neighborhood and visit our neighbors. Of course, they had costumes that were covered with their winter coats; we lived in Wisconsin. While my kids didn't get candy on a regular basis, they did get to eat some on Halloween. We always walked which meant we didn't get too much candy because when they were tired it was time to head home. Two places we always made sure we went to were Jadack's and Cherney's. I drove them to both of those places because of distance. Morie and Berdell Jadack lived south of the railroad tracks in the Village of Milladore, and they always gave out the regular size candy bars. You never got the mini candy bars from them; regular size only is what Berdell gave out. The second place was Francis and Bev Cherney who live out in the country about a mile from us. Bev had homemade caramels to give the kids. They were so soft and good, much better than the ones from the store.

One more story that needs to be recorded about Kevin was the fact that he was never going to be a farmer. When he was three years old, he told his Dad he was never going to run the farm for him. Ray assured him that he could run it himself. When I heard this back and forth discussion I asked Ray how it started; he couldn't tell me. Raymond always wanted to live on a farm, and his son knew at a very young age it wasn't going to be his life. Both of them had dreams for the future, and they were both going to be happy.

CHAPTER SIX

"Difficult roads often lead to beautiful destinations."
Unknown

When it was time for Valerie to start kindergarten, I knew I had to get someone to watch her in the Stevens Point school district because the bus would not pick her up outside the district. Judy and Ed Stashek had some renters in a house they owned that was next to their farm. I do not remember the woman's name, but Judy felt that she would do a good job taking care of Valerie and getting her on the bus. That woman had a child that was in Valerie's class. The first day she left for school she was actually at home because the picture I have on her first day was taken by Millie Younger. I didn't ask Millie to take the picture; she just offered; that was the kind of neighbor she was, always ready to help. Kevin was four years younger so I didn't have him go to the same babysitter; I had him in a home where there were small children closer to his age. Years later when Kevin was ready for kindergarten Julie Dickrell got him on the bus because her son Neal was in Kevin's class. Those boys had lots of fun in town because there were about four of them getting on the bus for afternoon kindergarten. Both of my kids had Miss Gumz as their first teacher, and they both enjoyed her. I know she liked my calm and reserved Valerie but my Kevin proved to be a handful. He started school on a Monday, and on Friday I went to school to check to see how he was doing. When I talked to Miss Gumz, she explained that he was better on that Friday. Apparently, she found him to be loud and active. That Friday the reason I went to school was that he had an earache and I didn't know if it was an infection or not; maybe we were going to have to make a trip to the doctors. Guess that ear issue made him a little quieter and less active.

When Valerie got home from school, her Dad would be in the barn, so I made books on tape for her to listen to before I was home. On Sunday night we would sit down together with four or five short books, and as I read them to her, we would use a tape recorder to record the stories. She would hold the books as I read and I would say "turn the page" just like the tapes we got from the library. Then Monday through Friday of the following week, she would listen to the tape as the books were re-read to her. This gave her something to do before I got home. When Kevin started school, this didn't work as well. He always wanted new books to listen to so about Tuesday he preferred to turn on the TV. I have no idea what he watched, but he could sit in front of the TV while Valerie was not interested in that form of entertainment.

Valerie's kindergarten class was preparing to go to visit the Stevens Point bakery. Miss Gumz asked if anyone's mother baked bread. My daughter told me about this, and she explained, "Some kids raised their hands." I knew we had to bake bread, so we made a trip to Mancl's in Milladore to purchase the frozen kind. While I didn't want to be the mom that just buys bread already sliced I wasn't going to start from scratch with the yeast and everything. We found what we needed in the frozen foods section. We put our frozen bread in a pan to let it thaw and rise through the night so we could bake it in the morning. That did make for a pleasant smell in the morning when I was trying to get the kids up.

Because of being born in the summer and going to school when he was just five, Kevin was one of the youngest students in his class. After his first day, I asked him how he liked it, and he explained that "You never want to be first." This was very strange because I knew how competitive he was even at that young age. When asked him to explain further he said, "First holds the door, you just want to be second." I had just started teaching at an elementary school, and he was right, first holds the door for all the other kids in the class and then follows last. Both Kevin and I started new phases in our lives at the same time with me going to the elementary level and Kevin going to Kindergarten. His first day I was thinking about him getting on the bus for the first time because he was going in the afternoon to school. Just about the time he was getting to school I had a first grade class coming into my gymnasium that I was meeting for the first time. My younger students were asked to walk in a single file and sit in a circle to listen to the directions for that day. As I was walking behind my little guys, one student looked just like my son from the back. I had to contain myself, so I didn't pick him up and ask why he was here because this was the wrong school. Troy didn't look like Kevin from the front as much as he did from the back. I can't remember Troy's last name but he always reminded me of my son, and I had him in my class until he went to Junior High as a seventh grader.

Going to first grade was another new experience for my kids because school lasted for the entire day. When Kevin went to first grade, it was the last time I needed babysitters while I was at work. Raymond commented, "That means more money for me." With that thought in mind, I decided to get someone to clean my house while I was at work. I talked to Deb Perkl, the first grade teacher at one of my schools and asked how she liked having a person clean her house for the year. Deb explained that she only had a person during the nine months she was in school because she didn't like someone cleaning while she was home. My solution was to leave during the summer months which gave me time to do things with the kids.

Valerie's first-grade teacher was expecting a baby when she was in her class. I had each child make a square for a quilt that I sewed together for the teacher. I don't remember having much of a problem getting all of her classmates to complete their square. We used quilting makers, and I am sure I had the help of the school secretary, Mary Malick. Valerie helped to tie the quilt and was so pleased to present it to her teacher. That was before I knew about machine quilting that does a better job to finish off a quilt. It makes all quilts stronger and neater when completed.

Later when Kevin was in first grade, I was trying to get to his Christmas concert on time with little time to spare. To attend Valerie's activities during the day; it was easier to get away when I was at the High School, but teaching at the elementary level made it more difficult. When I finished my last class in Marshfield, I only had 30 minutes before Kevin's program would start because his class would perform first. As I walked into Kennedy school, I heard everyone clapping which meant the first class had completed their performance. I dashed into the gymnasium to add to the clapping and Kevin saw me as he was coming off the stage. He had no idea that I had not been there the entire time. I was then able to relax and enjoy the rest of the concert which included Valerie's class about 35 minutes later.

Because Valerie's birthday was in early December, we had Santa Claus come with her birthday presents, and he told her and Kevin to be good because he would be back on the twenty-fifth of the month. Rudy Younger was our Santa, and I don't know what year he started, but he would walk across Highway 10 and often stop traffic as people were passing our home. I had purchased a Santa suit for him to wear and he dressed at home and walked to our place. Millie would drive over to stop by and say hi just about the time Jolly St. Nick arrived. Santa would leave the gifts and Rudy would join us in the living room to see our two kids open their presents. Rudy would just take the suit off in the back entrance and leave it on the washing machine. My objective would be to put it away before Valerie or Kevin saw the red suit.

Both my kids could swim by the time they went to school at age five. At one point I wasn't sure Kevin would ever learn to swim, he just didn't relax and float. Once after I was talking to my sister Pat, she told me that her daughter, Kim just put her face in the water and started swimming. Kim is about four months older than Kevin, but she was smaller in stature. When I told him that Kim had started swimming his comment was, "That little girl?" The next time we were at the pool, he stuck his head in and started swimming. Kim & Kevin were always competitive. Years later when they were older, and we took them for a day at Noah's Ark they were trying to decide who had done the best flip over the water and entering feet first. Pat and I were walking behind them and heard, them talking. "Mine was better." "No mine was better." After that, they were going to consult their mothers, but mothers can't be objective. My kid is always the best at everything, so we were no help.

While I was teaching at the elementary level in Marshfield, I no longer had the keys to the high school so we couldn't use the swimming pool at night or on weekends. We joined the YMCA in Marshfield which gave us more opportunities to take classes, and I put the kids in swimming lessons. There was also childcare available, but I didn't use it a lot because my kids were with a babysitter all week and I wanted to spend my time with them. There were a few classes that we attended together that offered something for all three of us. When I was teaching at the elementary level, I tried to get my workout done during my day of teaching. This was because it set a good example for my students to see me exercising along with them. There were also art classes at the "Y" to make things that we could use for the fair when submitting projects in 4-H.

Because I didn't want my kids to miss out on anything they were in 4-H, Boy Scouts, and Girl Scouts plus they participated in anything the grade school offered in the way of activities after school. The activities depended on the teachers involved and what their interests were. There were lots of different sports opportunities which both Val and Kevin enjoyed. A few times there were art projects offered because an art teacher was new and wanted to promote an area they enjoyed. Summer school was available, and I had them take a typing class one year because I wanted to get a computer and but back then I believed that you should not work on a computer until you could type. That class was so popular it was offered by lottery, but both my kids' names were drawn, so they learned to type during the summer of 1985. There were projects made in Scouting that could also be used in 4-H if they were in the right 4-H project. I was always looking for ideas or projects that could be used in both to save time and energy. Romelle Bymers gave me the idea of combining the projects from Scouts and 4-H. She was a student of mine during the first year I taught, and now she was a teacher at Madison elementary where I was teaching. She had been a 4-H leader for many years, and I am sure she still works with 4-H youth as a retired teacher.

Another time my kids won something at Kennedy elementary was when the school was selling jackets as a fundraiser for the school. When the slips to order were presented to me both of the kids were interested in ordering a jacket with the Kennedy logo on the back and their name on the front. Our family purchased two jackets. If you got your money in on the first day your name was tossed in a hat to get a free jacket. We won that free jacket, which made the secretary happy because she later said we were the only family to order two coats. She told me I could have my money back for one of the coats I ordered, but I told her to offer the coat to someone else that she knew would enjoy it. Money was never a big issue when I was working, and the farm was paying its way. I never inquired who got the free jacket, but I knew Mary Malick would find an individual that would appreciate it.

Second grade was a good year for Valerie; actually, she did very well all through her grade school years because she worked hard and paid attention to her teachers. The reason I mention second grade was because of spelling. Every Friday a spelling list was sent home, so you had a week to practice to take the test the next week. We worked on that list all week, and on Friday she never got a single word wrong. She usually knew the words by Wednesday and would be ready for the test; she is still a good speller. While in Kennedy Valerie joined the Girl Scouts which gave her many opportunities to work on projects and earn patches. She liked to read what was expected of an individual to obtain the patch and we would come up with ideas and activities. Later when she joined 4-H, as I mentioned earlier, we found we could do one project and use it for both organizations. She could earn a patch and keep the project for the fair in Marshfield to win a ribbon. Valerie did enjoy going to school at Kennedy in Junction City; the children were from wonderful families. and I don't ever remember students having to deal with bullying issues.

Maybe it happened, but kids were able to deal with it and move on; they didn't run to their parents to fix a problem that could just as easily be ignored.

About the time Kevin entered second grade it was determined that he needed glasses. His cousin, Mark Steines got his about the same time. When the eye doctor told Mark to wear them for reading, he only wore them in reading class until he was enlightened. Kevin was no better and didn't like wearing glasses. They came home a few times in pieces with a note from his teacher, Mrs. Zellner; telling me how sorry she was. It really wasn't her fault; she tried to remind him before going out to recess that he should take them off. Once when she missed him on the way out, he told me he put them down close to a pole. He demonstrated how close a person would have to be in order to break them by stamping his foot around an imaginary pole. It got better as he got older and I did get him contacts when he was in Junior High because he never did like wearing glasses or was able to tolerate them. Both of my kids got glasses about the same time but Kevin was the one that picked them up as soon as he got out of bed, Valerie could function without them.

Just before Christmas when Kevin was in second grade, and Valerie was in sixth, he came home with the idea that he wanted to be the one to provide a treat for his class. His teacher had asked if anyone could provide a treat. When Valerie heard about the idea of taking a treat to school for Christmas, she agreed it would be a great idea that they both take cookies or whatever treat I would like to make. I tried to fight it but Kevin could be persistent so I agreed, and I sent a note the next day with both kids to explain we would be happy to provide a treat for the class. When they came home from school Val's teacher said OK, and Kevin's teacher sent me a note explaining that they wanted a "tree," not a "treat." She asked if I would be getting a tree. We did; Valerie took rice crispy treats while Kevin took a tree. Kevin's went in early December so they could decorate it, while we had a few weeks to make Val's treats closer to the Christmas break.

Going to teacher conferences did prove to be interesting every year when the kids would get a new teacher. Valerie's only issue was organization. She was not able to keep her desk clean, and I often got a call that we owed money for lunches.

I was sending a check with her but sometimes it was a day late and then she would forget to tell the teacher on Tuesday that she had a check. That issue was solved when Kennedy went to a computer system where you could pay ahead, and I found paying for the year worked the best. Conferences for Kevin presented a different problem. Talking too much to Mark Blenker was what I heard about at these meetings. Mark's mother, Bonnie suggested that Mark was the closest thing Kevin had as a brother. They were best of friends all through grade school and beyond and it was not possible to separate those two because of "reading groups." The boys were at the same reading level, so they had to be in the same reading class, which then put them in the same class all day long. They made it the teacher's cross to bear; it was no problem for them.

We were not a wrestling family meaning no one had been in wrestling from Ray's family, and on my side, only my brother Albert had participated. He was already out of school and working before Kevin was born, so he had not seen Albert wrestle. The reason Kevin considered wrestling was because of Mark, he was from a wrestling family, so Kevin was hooked. Valerie enjoyed watching any sport where her classmates participated and if her brother was in the activity that was even better. Kevin started in second grade, and as I was driving him to the first match, he explained that the only thing he knew how to do was pin a guy. "Guess that is what you have to do then," was Valerie's contribute. That is just what he did, pinned the little guy and made him cry. I never did enjoy that sport even when Kevin was winning. Once when he was ahead in points I couldn't see his head, it was tucked under the other guy's body, but Kevin was winning. FYI, Valerie didn't participate in sports but enjoyed watching any events at Kennedy as well as SPASH.

About the time Kevin was in fourth grade he and Valerie were both helping Ray in the barn and receiving a salary from Ra-Con Farm. They were taught that you don't spend all your money but put some in the savings account at the bank, once in the savings account the money was not used to spend on things like Guess jeans. Kevin needed a pair of Guess jeans which were much more expensive than the twenty-dollar pair I was willing to purchase. Using my twenty and saving some of the money he was allowed to spend he purchased a pair of Guess jeans. At the same time, he wore his hair in a spike using mousse which was all the rage. Getting ready for school was a real project because he also needed a comb in his back pocket to hold the t-shirt up which couldn't be tucked in at the waist. The purpose of the comb was to allow the Guess triangle logo to be seen. Imagine how disappointed he was after getting ready for school one winter morning only to find it was called off for a snow day. Most kids would have been delighted, but he was dressed "cool" and had no place to go and was hugely disappointed because his efforts would not be noticed. I noticed, but that just wasn't enough.

When Valerie was in Mrs. Zellmer's class, other parents said they didn't want their children in her classroom because she was so strict. I never played that game of deciding which teacher my kids should have during the years they were in school. It turned out that Mrs. Zellmer was perfect for Valerie. As a teacher, she was very kind and understanding of the children in her classroom. Judy Stashek said her children also enjoyed Mrs. Zellmer as a teacher. It is best not to listen to rumors and make up your own mind about people.

There was a time when I could have considered no longer working off the farm, but I knew I would pick up new responsibilities working on the farm. This was of no, or at least, little of interest to me. I enjoyed teaching and knew the work on the farm would never end. Teaching gave me a beginning to my day as well as an end; leaving me to deal with my family and home after the school day ended. Besides once we stopped to think about it, if I did quit teaching our health insurance would be gone, and that would have been another bill for the farm to cover. Another thing about teaching, I enjoyed the interaction with my students and colleagues, something I would find hard to replace on the farm. Don't get me wrong; I enjoyed being with my husband but not 24/7.

When Valerie was fourteen and Kevin was ten years old we decided to take a family vacation and headed for Disney in Florida. I didn't want to plan a vacation like that until I knew my kids could pack for themselves and carry their own luggage. We did a great job getting ready for that trip because we were able to do it all as carry-on. When we were checking in for our flight the gal at the counter said she was impressed. I knew we were staying at the same motel for the week and they had a laundry, I just did a load of wash every second day, and we were golden. Besides all we needed was shorts and the kids wanted to purchase t-shirts, so we didn't take anything extra. I don't think I have ever packed that good since. That trip went so smooth, the car rental, the entrance fees, the motel location, all were perfect. Again, I don't think we have ever had a trip go that good since that time.

Just before we were leaving on that trip Kevin, was caught up in a "mooning" issue on the bus. When I asked him about the situation, he explained that he was an observer, not a participant. The parent that reported the event had my son's name on the "naughty" list. Getting in trouble on the bus is easy for boys that are bored and the only adult present has their back to them. I say, boys because my Valerie never had an issue. But back to Kevin, he was not going to be disciplined until we returned from Florida, so we went on vacation. Upon returning all the boys from the bus incident were called to the principal's office. Jerry Corgiat, the principal at the time told me that the first thing the boys said when asked was that Kevin wasn't involved. He was there to watch the action. Not the first or last time my son was "just living on the edge."

My two children were very different; an introvert would be my Valerie while the term extrovert would define my Kevin. We saw evidence of this truth when Kevin was dancing with a classmate of his, Leslie Linzmeier. Valerie enjoyed watching her little brother and Leslie perform, but she was not interested in participating. Leslie and her sisters had been in a dance club for years and for Leslie to be in the cowboy/cowgirl dance she needed to get a male partner. She asked Kevin, and he was willing to try it.

In Girl Scouts, Valerie worked hard to get different badges. When they completed a badge, the girls would report to others what they had learned and needed to do to earn a badge. Many of the other girls were willing to work with Valerie and get a badge together. Kevin also enjoyed getting badges in Cub Scouts and his finest hour was the Pine Wood Derby race. He and his father worked on turning a hunk of wood into a racing machine. That event was many years ago, but I know my kid's car was first.

When my kids were in grade school, they started to help Raymond with the evening chores. One would go to the barn while the other one stayed in the house to get homework completed. Every other night was your night, and they would exchange nights if someone had lots of homework. Planning, also worked if you were using your head to think and not just as a hat rack. They both were able to complete their homework with the extra time spent in the barn. Raymond would talk to the child that was in the barn with him and would find out more than I usually did. "Do you have the notebook Val needs for tomorrow?" Or, "did you pick up construction paper for Kevin?" were just a few questions I would get from Raymond when he got in at night. Most of the time I had what the kids needed, or I found out once they talked to their Dad. He is a better listener than I am.

These early years when my children were in grade school was when I completed my Master's degree at the University of Wisconsin-Stevens Point. Lots of classes were completed during the summer. The license plate I had on my car said: "GYM 581" which is referred to as a vanity plate. It was just the luck of the draw that I had completed my Masters in May of 1981, and I taught Physical Education or gym as some people refer to my subject area. I think that plate was on my yellow Cadillac which Raymond bought me when I wanted a Corvette. He told me the Cadillac was more practical because at least it had a back seat. He is always so good to me.

One last note about the days my kids were in elementary school was the time we took a vacation in Wisconsin Dells. We were in our Lincoln Town Car. That was a nice riding car which we had for more than ten years. While in the Dells we saw an advertisement for helicopter rides which the kids wanted to try. As we headed up the hill toward the place, there was another Town Car following us. Once we heard about the price of the rides, we decided that the two kids could go and we would wait for them. I don't remember the cost, but we were saving money. The people in the other Town car did the same thing; the kids flew while the parents waited. Does this say something to you about how much money a person has when driving a Lincoln Town Car? To me, it says my husband found me an excellent used car to drive.

My memories of the days my kids were at Kennedy school in Junction City are very delightful. All of the teachers were so good to my kids, and I was pleased with the education they received. It was more comfortable having them in Junction City while I was in Marshfield, but that was going to change when they headed to Junior High.

CHAPTER SEVEN

"Life is a journey we must pursue without a map."
Unknown

This chapter would have had a different outcome if I had gotten my wish to be the first private citizen in space. President Ronald Reagan announced in 1984 that the first person of the Space Flight Participant Program would be a teacher. His idea was that the communications back to earth would include lessons presented by a teacher while in space. I went as far as getting an application, but it was never submitted. There were more than eleven thousand other educators that applied for the position. The thing that stopped me from actually applying was the idea I would not be home at night with my family. I liked my job from eight to four and enjoyed the evening with my husband and kids. Also, my thought was that the perfect applicant would be a science teacher. Once I saw the length of the form and started to think about what I would miss in the lives of my family I decided I would not apply. I quit before I even started, but in light of the Challenger disaster, it wasn't my worst decision. Where were you on January 28, 1986, when

Christa McAuliffe and six others were launched into space? I was in the Lincoln gymnasium teaching a class when the music teacher, Edie Lauterbach walked through and asked if I had heard about the launch. She said, "They blew up." I said, "You mean they went up." I knew that some of our classes would be watching the story unfold live while it was being taped for others to view later in the day. It gave me a sick feeling knowing McAuliffe, a social studies teacher with two small children ages five and nine would never be presenting lessons from space. It was a sad day in our nation. A few months later McAuliffe's alternate was named, but I don't think the program was continued as it was planned, so the alternate never went into space.

Ben Franklin Junior High was the next step on Valerie and Kevin's educational journey, but they were never at the school together because they were four years apart in school and only seventh, eight, and ninth grades were at the junior high. When Valerie started in seventh grade she didn't get the idea of going back to her locker between classes; she would carry all her books to her classes. When one of her teachers realized what she was doing, we came up with a plan. That was a hefty load, so we reviewed the path she took to her classes. We wanted to have her go to her locker when she was walking close or right past it and have her stop to change books. We worked out a system for her, and she was still able to get to class on time. She wasn't the only student that had a problem with this, and the solution was easy once she realized she didn't have to be the first person to arrive for a class. She was never late for a class which made her happy. This is my Valerie, always a happy camper with a positive attitude.

Kevin never was as concerned about getting to class on time, because he didn't bother to carry all his books as his sister had tried years earlier. Because the two of them were so far apart in age, only a few teachers realized he was Valerie's brother. This also could have been because they followed different educational paths. They did both take a class in Family and Consumer Education. I don't remember Valerie having to do the project of sorting, washing, drying, folding and putting her clothes but then she never complained. It wasn't that Kevin complained about the project, it was just that he asked me to sign a paper stating he had sorted his clothes and continued with the project ending with them being put in his drawers. I stated that my signature on this form meant he had done all of the above as he said, "You're going to make me do this." "Yes, if you want me to sign it," was my reply. It got signed so he was able to complete yet another task that not only made him better but stronger. Just go with it, it sounds good and that is one of the many reasons for education.

Valerie never complained about the bus ride while Kevin had nothing good to say about it. For her, it must have been an opportunity to relax, and to him, it was a waste of time. Read a book was my suggestion which was not possible according to my kids. Once in a while one of them tried to complete a homework assignment, but we were usually able to get those finished the night before they were due. One would go out to the barn to help Dad while the other one helped me with the dishes and started their homework. Those barn chores were again approached differently by my two children. Valerie would do it just because mom said and it would please her father. Kevin just completed the task and would have been happy if the opportunity to go to the barn never came around again. That changed when they participated in the dairy project in 4-H.

During the summer months we worked on 4-H projects; at times both my kids took 30 different projects, so it kept them busy during the summer. When we got the tags to identify the projects, putting them on the correct project was a big task in and of itself. After Valerie & Kevin identified their projects they wrote the tags out I would affix them to the proper projects. During the fair, I would take the fair book for that year around to see the projects that were on display. If there was a project area that didn't have lots of entries I encouraged my kids to get into that project the next year because there would be less competition. It usually worked because a few of the projects my kids did had little or no competition. Every year I wanted to take a picture of their ribbons and a few of the projects, but it only happened once. I hung all their ribbons up on the back of the couch and had them sit in front of them. They were hung in order blue, red, white, and pink. Valerie is sitting in a dress that she made and wore for a fashion show and is holding her cat, which was the grand champion that year. Kevin has a model airplane and a woodworking project on his lap, but he positioned himself in front of the pink ribbons which represented last place. Pink wasn't bad; one-fourth of the class had to receive a pink ribbon. If there were 20 entries; only four could get a blue ribbon. That is the way it is done in Wisconsin, but he wanted the pink ones out of the picture.

We had a 4-H family when my children were active in North County Line 4-H club. Hollar's with their ten children were active and helped my two with many project ideas. Mike and Sally Baltus' four children were active and Sally could come up with some of the best ideas. She found a radio contest for us to enter, which was so much fun. Think about it, there were no costumes to deal with; the kids wrote a script and we recorded the program. The kids had the most fun coming up with the sound effects. LeRoy and Leiann Altmann's family was also in our club; they were big in the animals that we showed for dairy. My two learned a lot about showing cattle from this family. Valerie also remembers Dan Miller helping the younger members to prepare or trim the animals for the show ring.

Valerie always loved to play sports, and when the necessary skill level was above her performance level, she turned to becoming the manager of a few of the teams. When she got bored with that, she became what I would call a "professional fan." Because an avid supporter of all the sports at Ben Franklin it didn't matter if it was a boys or girls team; she went to any home event. She could usually find someone to go with her, but if not, she would ask me. I remember one gymnastic meet no one was interested in going to so we were in the stands cheering for the Ben Franklin Chargers. It was one of the few times she and I went to see gymnastics. Basketball, swimming, or wrestling would have been her first choices, and she had friends interested in attending those events with her.

When Kevin got to Junior High, he was the one that wanted to participate. Because of my background in Physical Education, I did not want him to be in football. I think it was when he was in eighth grade when he was complaining that he couldn't go out for football. This wasn't the first time I heard these complaints. Years earlier I had taken a class with a group of coaches from Marshfield. We were learning about the ways to protect ourselves from being sued when a student is injured. Because many of the coaches had a football background, we dealt with many of football scenarios. I will never forget what the lawyer said before we concluded. "Look, you have the parents sign a disclosure that explains the safety equipment we are having your child wear, and he or she could still get hurt or killed." That isn't how the disclosure would read, but it was a lawyer speaking English, not complicated "lawyer speak." Because of that class, I didn't figure football was worth the effort. Let me say, I enjoy watching the Green Bay Packers but I didn't want my kid playing that game. I remember once when sitting with a group of football coaches complaining about their loss the night before our coffee clutch, all I said was, "it's only a game." Their reaction was deadly, and I backtracked as fast as I could. But back to Kevin and his issue of not being able to play football; I finally told him, "play football but don't come crying to me when you get hurt and can't play basketball." It worked he never played football, and I don't think he really wanted to play a game where you might never touch the ball during the entire game.

Kevin did participate in basketball and baseball for the years he was at Ben Franklin. We would have to look at the yearbooks to be sure, but I believe he was in those two sports all three years. He found that basketball was his sport and during his junior high career he seldom sat on the bench. The kid was able to stay in shape running up and down the court. At these younger grades, the theory was to have everyone get some playing time, and Kevin did get his share if not a little extra. Baseball was a different story; he didn't make the traveling team during the summer which gave him extra time to work on the farm. What he did do during the summer was set up a whiffle ball park and had the boys from town join him for a game. The park he set up was named Virgin Park because in the outfield stood a statue of the Virgin Mary. That statue was a birthday present for me from Raymond and Valerie before Kevin was born.

My two children had the opportunity to play softball in the Village park during the summer months. If I remember it correctly their night to play was Tuesday evening. The three of us would head to the ballpark together while Raymond would do the evening milking. If we were not home when Ray was finished milking after he cleaned up, he would come to the park to join us. There were different fathers that coached during the years Val & Kevin played at the park. I remember when Ray Linzmeier was coaching Kevin's team, his daughter Leslie was on the team. Ray put Kevin in the outfield because he was younger and needed more practice before he was ready for the infield. I spotted him in the outfield with a bag of potato chips. I told Ray to call him in to get his glove. Kevin knew it was my "idea" that he should have his glove. I am sure Mr. Linzmeier had other things to be concerned about during the game. Kevin explained his reasoning because he told me, "No one hits the ball to the outfield." That was one of the earlier years because Kevin did start when he was seven; during that summer, in July was his eighth birthday.

Another time when they were playing softball at the park, the sky opened, and it started pouring rain. Everyone headed for the shelter, and we were hoping it would clear so we could continue the game. Hal Richardson was standing by us, and we were discussing the situation. Raymond told him that it was supposed to clear, but it might take an hour or longer. Raymond always knows what the weatherman has been saying because he likes to review all updates. It started to rain even harder, and someone in the crowd yelled, "Play ball." All the little kids took off for the field, but Hal didn't move; he was the umpire for the game, but he was waiting for the rain to stop. The kids realized they had been tricked and returned to the shelter. We waited another ten minutes to make sure the field was going to be too wet to pl ball, then everyone headed to their cars, there would be another game the following Tuesday.

When my two children were helping Raymond in the barn on a regular basis, they were given a salary. As I recorded earlier, they could not spend all of the money but had to put some in the savings account. Once their savings accounts grew enough, I had them open a certificate of deposit or CD at the local bank. This was a good learning experience for them because they made the selection for the term. Both of them choose the longer option for the higher annual percentage yield or APY. At one point these CDs came due, and they had to be renewed. We went to the bank and talked to Sally Furo about the new APY. The kids had been getting 7% while their Dad was paying 18% on his loan. Both interest rates were going down so what the kids were going to get on the renewed CDs, even if they went for the longest term was less than the 7%. Kevin explained that he was happy with the 7% not the 3% Sally was going to offer him. Sally just smiled and explained she couldn't provide that 7% today, but Kevin didn't understand that his Father was now getting a better deal on his farm loan.

Valerie and Kevin learned another vital lesson from receiving wages for working on the farm. Because of their earnings, we had them file a tax return. Once when Kevin was signing his return, he was reviewing it and saw that it told him he had earned over $3000 during the year. He wanted to know where all the money was, so we took the time to review his accounts as well as Valerie's. The CDs were the same amount for both of them, but Kevin's checking account didn't have as much as Valerie's. She was a saver, and Kevin was a spender, and when a spender looks back on what they purchased, there doesn't seem to be much to show for the money spent. Have you ever tried just reviewing what you have after a day of shopping? For me, I find the review daunting and wonder what I thought when I purchased all the items I have to put away. Is that called buyer's remorse?

When we planned our Florida trip, I took the kids to the bank to purchase traveler's checks. Today, about thirty years later we would be purchasing a travel card which looks like a credit card. They both took one hundred dollars from their savings account and purchased five twenty-dollar checks. The purpose of getting their own money was to buy souvenirs for themselves. When we arrived in Florida before we even left the airport, Kevin needed a hat. I told him to take one of his checks and sign it. After thinking about it, he decided he would wait. His first purchase was a pair of mirror sunglasses that was a perfect fit for his little head, while Valerie waited until she found a Florida t-shirt. At one point the kids had not spent much money, and we were getting low, so we had them each buy breakfast one morning. Valerie was old enough that she had to eat from the adult menu, but Kevin could order from the kid's menu. He did not want to order from the kid's menu until it was his turn to pay, then he could see an advantage to ordering from that menu because of the lower cost.

About the time Valerie was leaving Junior High, I came up with the bright idea that she should start mowing our lawn with the riding mower. Ray felt Valerie should wait until she was a little older. I finally convinced him into letting her mow because in a few short years the state of Wisconsin was going to let her drive on the road. There would be traffic coming toward her and learning to control a mower would be easier. It was nice having an extra person to do the riding while I did the trimming. Kevin is fours years younger but the next summer he was ready to get on the mower. It didn't take long for the activity to lose its appeal but I never mowed the lawn again unless there was a kid on the rider. The only thing that was an issue was when I would do the trimming there was more to do because I didn't let them mow as close as I did. But it was nice in the summer sun, and I have always enjoyed the look of my lawn after being mowed. There is nothing better than the smell of a newly mowed lawn unless Ray was baling hay, nothing can compete with the scent of fresh hay.

In August of 1985, we had a Mass at our farm. Father John Wisneski had an altar he used to say Mass in the Milladore Park during the summer months. I think that altar was made by Father Berg and he would say the Saturday evening Mass in the Park during the summer. Father John asked if we would consider having the Mass at our farm on August 15, for the Assumption. He felt with our farm less than a mile away it would be easy for people to find. In the church bulletin, we asked people to bring lawn chairs. What we did was place a half circle of straw bales toward the back for those that didn't have a chair. That half circle was a mistake because everyone that brought chairs placed them behind the bales leaving a large void between the altar and the congregation. It didn't bother Father John because he explained it isn't a lot different in church. We tried to get as many people as possible involved in the Mass. We asked Glenn Hartman to do a reading even though he isn't Catholic. Father John was pleased to have lots of individuals involved. We were delighted with the attendance, but then we did have beautiful weather.

In 1985 the band known as Starship wrote the song, "We Built This City." I always called it, "We Built This City on Rock 'N Roll," but I added the second line of the song to the title. That band went on tour and was going to be at the University of Wisconsin-Stevens Point campus. I don't remember the year, but they had come out with another hit which Valerie and Kevin enjoyed, so they just had to go. They don't remember the name of the second song, and I have done some searching on the internet but can't find the one that fits our timeline. But back to the story, I had to take them, and the deal was we all purchase our tickets using our own money. I tried to talk them into the idea that they should pay for my ticket because I wasn't that interested in attending. That idea didn't work, but it was just a thought. In the car, on the way to Stevens Point we heard both of the songs, and when Starship got on stage, their first song was "We Built This City." The next song was the current popular hit the kids wanted to hear, and it was so loud that when that song was completed, I asked them if they were ready to leave. They were more than willing to head for the door. As we were leaving, I saw a sign above the door where we had entered that said, "This concert may cause hearing loss." Unreal, if you ever attend a concert consider wearing ear protection. Do you understand why it has to be so loud?

When we were farming Raymond tried to update his equipment when he could afford it. At one point he got a kicker baler. It saved us from needing two people to go to the field when we were trying to bale hay. When the kids were in junior high, they could help unload but loading a wagon, while in the field took a much bigger and stronger person on the wagon behind the baler. Once Kevin went with Yogi Mancl, they were making hay for Clarence Hamus. Kevin must have been the driver and Yogi was the muscle needed to load because their baler was the not a kicker, so there was a need for two people to make hay. Yogi was laughing at Kevin when he explained that his father had one of those balers when he, Kevin was just a kid. Yogi felt Kevin was still just a kid. After the two of them had been working for a few hours, Clarence came out with a beer and a pop for them. He handed Kevin the beer and Yogi got the soda. After a taste, Yogi realized something was wrong because the Clarence had promised him a beer. Seeing Kevin's grin Yogi switched cans with the comment, "I didn't drink much."

Our kicker baler was not the most natural thing to learn to use. When I was sent to the field with that baler, I not only had to drive but had to get two settings right to get a bale into the wagon. The wagons had three ten-foot sides with the fourth front one only about three feet high. When we got that baler, Mike Baltus showed me where to disengage the arm of the kicker, and he told me never to be behind the baler if it was not disengaged. He explained that the arm would break your jaw if it didn't kill you. That arm was made to toss a fifty to sixty-pound bale of hay into the air about five feet. That takes lots of power and could hurt a person. So I learned to disengage the arm when getting behind the baler to unhook or hook up wagons. When I was baling across the road on Rudy Younger's farm, he would come to the field and watch as I baled. He would be there to help me change wagons. Once he and Valerie were both there watching me bale. Valerie enjoyed being outside, and Rudy was there as the supervisor. She was too small to disengage the arm but enjoyed Rudy's company, and he took care of that chore. Once when I had the wagon just about full, and I was at the far end of the field, I decided to turn the kicker up to have the bales land in the back of the wagon. I saw Valerie's reaction as the bale was kicked up and thought it was hitting the wagon. When I got back to Rudy and Val, I turned the wagon just a bit and could see I had a neat row of eight bales on the ground. I asked Rudy if any of the bales had stayed on the wagon. With a smile, that one could call a smirk; he said, "Not a one." I read Val's reaction as one a delight because I got a bale to stay on the wagon, but she was disappointed. I had just turned the dial up too high, and the bales were not real heavy, so they sailed over the wagon. Ray and I discussed who should pick those bales up. "If I pick them up," he explained, "you won't learn to be more careful." Let it be said there was more discussion about this issue. I was helping him, and it was not easy to learn how to make all those adjustments because the weight of the bale had to be considered. Enough said. I was his best helper because I worked for nothing.

As I wrote before, my kids both got glasses when they were in grade school. Through the years Valerie didn't need them, and she would seldom put them on when she got up in the morning. Kevin was a different story; he put them on when

getting out of bed and never missed an opportunity to tell me how much he hated wearing them. When he was in Junior High, I'm not sure how it started, but he began a campaign for contacts. I didn't like the idea because of my concern for him taking care of them. Finally, I let him try, and he didn't have any significant issues. I don't remember him ever losing one or misplacing them. Years later I decided to try them. Contacts are better than glasses because I am always losing my glasses when I take them off. I don't need them to see far, and only look for glasses if I am reading.

Before the kids headed to SPASH Tim and Donna lived less than six miles from our farm. Our kids would play together while we were working in the field. Donna made the observation that Kevin and Valerie were so patient and kind when teaching her kids to play softball. We had a batting tee that made it possible for the younger kids to hit and there was no need for a pitcher. Kevin would point the batter in the correct direction of first base after a hit. Tim and Donna's third child, Jon was our Godchild. When Donna asked Ray and me to be his sponsors, she told me he was going to be baptized Lutheran. She asked if that would be OK because we are Catholic. I told her if it was OK with her minister it was OK with me. I never asked our priest who was Father John Wisneski at the time. Imagine our surprise when we arrived at the church to see that there was another baby being baptized, and the Godmother for that child was Martha Mancl, a member of our church. Martha had been a CCD student of mine and her mother, Joyce Mancl was the housekeeper for our parish priest. Long story short; three of the four sponsors that day at St. John's Lutheran Church in Auburndale were Catholic. Of course Father John heard about it and was not upset. Joyce had asked about Martha standing up, and he felt it was just fine.

When it came time for Valerie to head to SPASH; Stevens Point Area Senior High, I was not ready to let her go. Mothers can't stand in the way of this kind of progress so off she went. A few years later when it was time for Kevin I realized we could live through another one at SPASH. It was time for my kids to get ready to take on the world, but I was looking for a non-existent map to help me guide them.

CHAPTER EIGHT

"Change your thoughts, and you'll change your world."
Unknown

When it came time for Valerie to move on to Stevens Point Area Senior High or SPASH, I was thinking she was getting comfortable with her surroundings at Ben Franklin. Then again, it might have been the fact that I was pleased with her being at the Junior High and I wasn't ready to have her go to SPASH. She graduated from SPASH in May 1991; while Kevin finished in 1995. His wife Sarah would complete her degree in 1996, and I think I did go to her graduation party; they might have started dating again when she was heading off to college at Green Bay. I know Nancy Michel always mentions that she wasn't invited to Kevin's graduation party, but they were not together at the time; not my fault.

Valerie was pleased with her time in high school. She joined many clubs and participated in as many activities as she could with the time she had in those three years. Val also enjoyed keeping scrapbooks of sports events while she was in school. Wonder if she has them yet? We had the Marshfield News-Herald and the Stevens

Point Journal coming to our mailbox every day. I needed the Marshfield paper to see what was going on in the city where I was teaching, and the kids needed the Journal because sometimes they were even in the newspaper.

One March I had to pick up a paper from Wisconsin Rapids. A photographer from that paper was driving through Milladore on US Highway 10 when he spotted a group of boys playing basketball at the home of Leonard and Dawn Hassel. The caption which appeared below a picture that he took said, "March madness in Milladore." The basket hoop was put up for Leonard's grandson who had a group of boys playing a basketball game. Kevin was part of that group. When he came home that afternoon, he told me I had to get a copy of the Rapids paper because he might be in it. Great, now I needed three papers to keep up with my kids. I don't remember if someone gave me a copy or if I purchased a paper but I saved it because Kevin was making a perfect jump shot in the picture. He thinks he made that basket, was what he told me. I am sure he did because that jump shot looked great. The photographer got all the boys names for the picture. On that same day, Valerie was attending a University of Wisconsin-Stevens Point hockey game in New York. Her picture appeared in the New York paper as the group of students was entering the hockey rink. She and a few of the other spectators were carrying signs to support the team. She was able to get a copy of the paper dated the same day as her brother's jump shot debut. What are the odds of that happening? I had to put those two pictures in a scrapbook to keep for posterity. If you are wondering about the date it was March of some year; I have been looking for that scrapbook for a few months now knowing this chapter was going to be written, but I have yet to find it. I know I will locate it because I don't toss things that are important to me.

Kevin also enjoyed his high school career, and SPASH was the perfect setting for him because it gave him an introduction to a larger school. I feel that a smaller high school would have been OK for Valerie but Kevin had to branch out. Both of them enjoyed SPASH because there were so many activities that were of interest to them. When Valerie went to the high school, she met lots of new friends because there were not many students from Milladore that were her age. Kevin kept his

Milladore friends and added a few more. It just happened that there were more kids his age in Milladore when he was in school. It seemed that when I had to drive them to a friend's house that friend usually lived on the other side of Stevens Point. When they were in Junior High, there were two junior highs where the students all went to one high school. The junior high, Ben Franklin that my two attended had the students from Kennedy in Junction City, and the rest of the school population came from the far side of Point. The students for the other junior high came from the city population. It wasn't until they got to the high school that they finally had friends that didn't live quite so far from us.

Once they started driving it was no longer a concern of mine if I didn't have to do the driving. When Valerie got her learner's permit to drive, we volunteered at the hospital in Marshfield which gave us a reason to drive to Marshfield, and it gave her some practice time. I know just before her first test, I told Raymond she wasn't ready for it because she drove with too much hesitation. He thought she should try and that would give her some experience taking the test. The first time she did fail; going too slow and just not demonstrating lots of confidence was the issue. But the second time when she came back from that driving test I could see from the smile on her face, she had passed. I almost cried, my baby was growing up too fast, and now the state of Wisconsin was going to let her drive. Jerry Fuehrer told me once that he was following a line of cars coming from Stevens Point going to Milladore, and when he got to the front of the line by passing those cars, he realized Valerie was the one going so slow to create the line. She was obeying the speed limit. If the posted speed limit is 55 miles per hour and you put your car on cruise at that speed, you will have a line of cars behind you unless you are on a double-lane highway. And if you are on a double lane highway going the posted limit, there will be cars blowing past you. I have not always driven like my daughter, but a few years ago I got a ticket, and I told Raymond that was like feeding a dead cow. There is no profit, and it is better to save money on gas by slowing down and obeying the speed limit. I still have trouble with the speed limit in town when it is 25 MPH. That is very slow, and the cruise doesn't even work at that speed.

Kevin played basketball and baseball when he was at Ben Franklin and SPASH. At first, there were a few other boys from the Milladore area that were on the teams so our families could share rides when getting the boys from practice. At times I had to meet a family in Junction City who would bring Kevin that far so I didn't have to go all the way to Point. Once when I got to Junction City early while I was waiting for him, I went for a jog. As our neighbor, Bev Cherney drove by me I just waved. Bev had gone to SPASH for her daughter Rhonda and thought they should check to see if I was OK. Rhonda was sure I had not flagged them down but was only waving to say, "Hi." She was right; I was just getting some exercise. This is what it means to live in a small town; people take time to check on each other. Like I wrote before, that wasn't the first time I was jogging, and someone stopped to ask if I needed a ride. Hal Richardson, our milkman at the time checked as I was heading to the Milladore Village Park to watch my kids play softball. Later he talked to me and said, "Now you do that for exercise, and I should drive by without stopping, right?" Small town USA, this is where people care about each other.

When it came time for Kevin to take his driving test, the story was different than Valerie's experience. When he had just his learner's permit, he got a parking ticket and locked his keys in a car before he even received his license. During June of the summer he turned sixteen he didn't drive to the University of Wisconsin-Stevens Point where he and some of the boys were taking a basketball workshop; it was Jeff Wright that drove and parked the car where Kevin felt it would work. So maybe the parking ticket wasn't his, but it was the car owned by Raymond. The keys were locked in at Fleet when he drove me there to pick up something for Raymond. While we were in the store, Kevin realized he didn't have the keys. Yes, the bell was going off as he got out of the car but he ignored it. Was I supposed to tell him to take the keys? After we got past all of that, we did some driving coming home from basketball practice during the week. When he played basketball during his sophomore year, there was no one to share rides with because the other local kids were in different sports or had not continued with basketball. When I finished teaching in Marshfield, I would drive home to start supper or do some other chores and then head to Stevens Point to pick up Kevin from practice. When he had his temporary license to drive, he then had the opportunity to drive home, which gave him lots of practice time.

Because he had just about a year of driving when he took his test, he passed on his first try. We were in Stevens Point to take the test, and I knew he was ready for it. What a shame, the state of Wisconsin was willing to recognize him as a driver, and he never rode the bus again. He always hated the bus ride because, according to him, it was a total waste of time. Sometimes, I think it would be nice to have someone drive me everywhere, and I could be writing or something. I do listen to books on CD, and I get through lots of books that way. At issue is when the book/CD is getting to a good part, this is when I find my drive isn't long enough, but it isn't like I would want to drive further to work or back home, I was OK with a 25-minute drive each way when I was teaching.

Once Valerie had her license she didn't drive every day to school; she would take the bus if she didn't have something after school that required her to stay late. The biggest issue with driving to school was getting the car registered to park in the student lot at SPASH. I don't recall either of my kids getting a ticket for parking during school hours so we must have been able to get the vehicles registered. I think when Kevin was a senior the permits to park were going to be issued on a lottery system. That parking lot doesn't have unlimited space, and every other student drove a car. If you ever took the time to look at the vehicles, very few were beaters like we drove when I was in high school.

Kevin had many friends in Milladore as I have mentioned before; 1977 was the year of many boys born in our small town. He was the youngest in his age group but had more confidence than most. It wasn't until his junior year that he started driving to school every day, and I did hear him complain once that he didn't like always driving at lunchtime, but his friends wanted to go out, so he felt obligated to take them. Life can be tough; it isn't like he had to put gas in the car using his own money. Both of my children had a credit card that was paid by me at the end of the month. It was a Ford credit card, and I could earn money off on my next new car. They did help me purchase a 1997 Thunderbird which

I didn't drive in the winter, so I never had an issue of rust while I owned it. As far as having money, both had an allowance because they did help their Dad in the barn or with fieldwork. Valerie enjoyed it more than Kevin. I remember once when Ray mentioned that Valerie would always ask if there was anything else to do before she went to the house, while Kevin never asked. I talked to him about that fact, and he explained he just left the barn when he was done with the chores he had been asked to complete. "Why not ask Dad if there was anything else," I inquired. "Because he'll give me something else to do," was the reply. Kids, they make life entertaining.

Valerie would do what she was told because that is the way it is supposed to be; parents tell kids what to do. It isn't like I was "bossy" I just knew what my kids were supposed to do and I told them. Kevin was another story, he might do what he was told, but there was always a question as to why is this necessary? CCD was a good example. Valerie never complained about attending CCD while in high school, but Kevin only wanted to go if his buddy, Mark was going. Once when he got home from school, on a CCD night, he picked up the phone and dialed. Few words, maybe less than 6, were spoken before he hung up. I had to ask him about the call. "I was just checking to see if Mark was going to CCD," was his reply.

For thirty-four years I taught CCD at St. Wenceslaus. My children had me only one year each; it was not easy for them because they were held to a higher standard with their mother as the teacher. It wasn't that big of an issue for Valerie, but it was for Kevin. His friends were good at reporting any of Kevin's shortcomings or failures to meet expectations. I know they were not trying to help me but trying to get him in trouble. In all honesty, he was like most of my students, basically excellent but challenging. On CCD nights, I am sure Raymond went to the barn alone because we had CCD and they had homework. Raymond did have help at times, but farming "with" him meant he did most of the work.

During the years that I had the confirmation class, I came up with a community project for them to do which was; clean-up a section of the highway going past the church. All confirmation candidates had to come up with a service project and the highway clean up was perfect. Around this time I was president of the Marshfield

Teachers' Association and because I lack creativity I came up with the same service project for them. Segments of the road were assigned in 2-mile lengths to any interested organization. Ra-Con farm also sponsored a 2-mile stretch along highway S from our farm to the north which Kevin used as his service project when applying for National Honor Society. If you are following, there were six miles of highway that our family would walk to pick up garbage. According to the rules for the project, two people are not supposed to be walking on both sides of the road when picking up trash. This was one of the rules that we didn't obey when picking up our farm's portion. Highway S isn't busy at certain times of the week, and we would often pick up on Sunday's after church when Ray went back to the barn to complete chores. The kids and I would pick up the junk and be careful not to be in a traffic accident. Still, against the law but at times we could walk a mile before seeing one car.

Dances and proms are other things I should write about for posterity. The first dance Valerie went to was a homecoming dance. The dresses were more like prom dresses than the winter outfits I wore to homecoming. Styles change, and a person just has to keep up. I remember one prom Valerie went to that I had her go with a friend to try on dresses. I did not send her with a credit card because I didn't want her to have a dress that we would have to return. I don't remember the reason I could not go with her, but I am sure it was my teaching career that was used as an excuse. She tried on many dresses and had taken pictures using a Polaroid so we could review them at home. I know none of her dresses were as inexpensive as my first prom dress. Mom and I found a beautiful dress for $9.00, and I wore it twice in high school and once in college. For one thing, my mother was the best when scoping our a good deal; I could never compete.

With Kevin it was so much easier, just rent a tux. I think he went to a prom or homecoming in Wisconsin Rapids. He wasn't old enough to drive, so I think Nathan Czaikowski was a cousin to Kevin's date, so the Czaikowski family drove. Kevin started dating Sarah during his junior year, and we have lots of pictures of dances and events they attended together. What does a person do with all these pictures? Now with the storage of online photos, they are easier to organize, and space isn't a big issue. For some reason, I still have pictures printed, and I enjoy putting them in scrapbooks. What does a person do with all of those books when I am gone? Not my concern, I made them to enjoy looking back at good times. FYI; I am writing this at a time when I will no longer allow myself to print another picture until I have all the current printed photos in an album. Sometimes to get myself moving on a project I have to get strict with myself.

I remember Joe Michel saying it seemed like Kevin and Sarah had been dating for years because Kevin had been at their home so much during the years they were dating. Once Sarah was waiting for Kevin to come and said something to her mother about him being late; Nancy informed her Kevin had arrived a while ago and was in the basement watching TV with Laura, Sarah's youngest sister. Yes, it was a big house that they had in Stevens Point. When he first met Sarah and saw where she lived, he commented to me about the Michel family being rich. Big house equaled rich in his mind back in those high school days.

Valerie never got a speeding ticket or totaled a car, but then there was Kevin. Valerie did get a ticket for going the wrong way on a one-way street. I just think she didn't have anyone in the car helping her navigate to find where they were going; they were in Rapids, and she didn't know the streets that well. Kevin was going to school on December 20, 1993, not me; Marshfield had called off because of the lousy winter weather. So when my vehicle came back in the yard, I thought Kevin had forgotten something. He came to the house to tell me the car pulling out of the yard was not mine. I asked him, "What is Nathan doing with my car?" He tried again to explain it wasn't my car, but I asked him again, and finally listened to the answer. He had been in an accident. Years later I found out he was supposed to be meeting Sarah Michel that morning in the library; the Lord had other plans for him. As the story goes; when they were leaving Milladore, Nathan said something about how bad the driving conditions seemed to be and decided to put on his seatbelt. Later I mentioned to him; he always needed to wear it when in my car. Kevin was not yet to Junction City when he came up behind a snowplow, the best place to be if it is snowing hard, but he decided to pass. It didn't work out as he had planned because his vehicle ended up on its side. After stopping, Nathan crawled up and out of the car but let the door drop. Kevin asked him why because he was planning to follow him out. Nathan explained he was coming around to help Kevin out. At issue was that car was lying on the driver's side; Nathan wasn't thinking clearly. Nathan then pulled his door open, and as Kevin was getting out, a car stopped to help them. It could have been the vehicle that came off the manufacturing line in the factory after mine. The two SUVs were identical. Kevin's thought was, the vehicle is OK, it didn't get damaged. Another person not thinking clearly; both of the boys were in shock. This was before everyone had a cell phone so the other driver offered to take the boys to a phone. As they headed back to Milladore, Kevin realized the best phone to use was ours, and we were only half a mile out of Milladore. What I did was call Hughes to get the car hauled back to town. As we were driving back to the scene of the accident I was telling the boys to stay in the car until the police arrived because of the icy conditions and I didn't want them to get hit. As I saw the car, I said to Kevin, "You didn't tell me it was on its side." "Don't you cry mom," was his reply. I could have lost him that day, but his guardian angel was taking care of him. That accident did slow him down, and it took a few years before he cared to drive in the winter. He learned the hard way that a 4-wheel drive vehicle doesn't help on ice.

There are so many stories about the time that my children were in high school, but at one point I just have to decide to finish the chapter. The rest of the stories might not be in chronological order, but I do want to get them on paper for posterity. Enjoy.

Once when I took Valerie and Kevin to a baseball game between DC Everest and SPASH, I was wearing a Packer shirt. As I went to sit down next to them, Valerie mentioned that I had the other team's colors on and that just wasn't acceptable. Again, I decided to get some exercise while waiting for them by going for a walk. I do enjoy walking, and I have never been the best spectator at games or events, just not enough activity. In those days I used a small hand-held tape recorder to listen to a book on tape while walking or jogging. When I had a good book, there was motivation to continue with the activity.

Valerie enjoyed hockey games and usually went with friends but once I took my two kids. It was my first game, and Kevin wanted to go because Jack Staskoff, a teacher he had in elementary was the coach. As soon as we arrived at the rink, I realized I should have dressed warmer than you do when attending a basketball game. That is "ice" they are skating on, and the arena has to be at a colder temperature. When the players skated off the ice for their first break, I went to the car to warm up and get a blanket to sit on for the rest of the game. During that break, Kevin went to the locker room to see his former teacher and the team. When he came back, he had a hockey puck. Valerie felt it was not fair; she wanted to go into the locker room too. There is a saying, "life isn't fair." The next time the team skated off the ice I stood up to put my coat on as Valerie asked why we were not staying for the end of the game. Oh, hockey has three periods, not like basketball with two halves. We stayed.

When Valerie graduated in May 1991, her class had 625 students graduating. Randy Meyer, who was on the school board in Loyal at the time told her that there were more students in her graduating class than in the school population in the Loyal School District. There were times that SPASH was considered the largest school in the state of Wisconsin. Both larger and small districts offer good programs for their students. I don't remember the size of Kevin's class in 1995, but I remember there were more students in his class; the actual number eludes me.

Both of the parties we had to celebrate their graduation were at Hamm's, our local pub. In the back, there was a large banquet hall which was perfect for our gathering. The one thing I learned at Valerie's party was cut the cake early. It is a shame not to let everyone see the beautifully decorated cake but if you wait to cut it people are gone, and you end up with lots of cake. I had her picture put on the cake, so I didn't want to cut it. For Kevin, we just had an ordinary cake because of the unique centerpiece. I used an old trophy and put a basketball shoe on it to be placed next to the cake. As the story goes, he didn't have two of those shoes only one. Let me explain; if you are on a basketball team, you need to have the "right" shoes. I am not sure who decides which of the many shoes the right ones are, but Kevin and I went to Wausau to purchase the right pair that all the other members of his team were getting. He tried them on in the store and found the perfect fit. I paid for them, and we headed home. When we arrived, he tried them on again and realized he had the wrong pair. He did have the pair that he had tried on in the store, but he didn't notice that they were not the "right" pair. Back to Wausau, we went the next day to return a perfect pair of black shoes that lacked one stripe and got the "right" pair. Every new basketball season we had to get a different pair even if last year's pair was in perfect condition, which it was because they were only worn on the basketball court and never outside. Once he came home, from an away game, he had only one basketball shoe. I called the school where they had played, but the lost shoe was never found. I don't know if we had to purchase another pair or if we went with last year's pair to finish the basketball season. The thing I do remember is I kept that one shoe and used it as a centerpiece for his graduation party. Hate to have a perfectly good shoe go to waste.

As I recall the years my two attended SPASH I believe they both enjoyed the experience. My prayer is that others enjoy their years in high school as much. I am at a loss when I hear about the shooting in our schools that have reached epidemic levels. Columbine did happen while I was teaching and it gave all of us as teachers pause to think of a student that would do something like that to get attention. There are no easy answers, and I don't believe the government can help us with the issue. Parents have to step up and "parent." We all need to change our thoughts on thinking the school can do it all for our children; parents have to do their part when raising their children.

CHAPTER NINE

"Don't be pushed by your problems. Be led by your dreams."
Ralph Waldo Emerson

As I re-read the last paragraph from the previous chapter I realized it made me sound like I was preaching, that might be the case but "for the grace of God, there go I." Both of my children had dreams or ideas of what they wanted from life, and I believe Raymond and I helped them as they were growing into young adults. Both of my children went on to higher education, which we did not save for while they were growing up. It was always the plan that I should continue to work to pay for their education. It didn't seem right to put money away when we had a debt on the farm. It was my objective not to have the kids incur debt that would have to be paid off when they completed their studies. Raymond and I were so lucky to be able to meet that objective. I always divided my paycheck in half; spending half and putting half in the savings. At one point Ray realized we had to stop borrowing if we ever wanted to be out of debt ourselves; thus he used the savings account when he needed something for the farm. Paying cash up front is better than borrowing money from the bank; see the bank needs to be paid back, the savings account not so much. Raymond never made the exact payment when sending money back to the bank. He often tried to make a double payment which made it hard at times, but by 2003 we had the farm paid off even with an 18% interest rate for a few years. It would have been paid for much earlier, but I had the farm pay for a "cute" red truck for myself as well as a house in Milladore. When I showed the place to Luella, she asked what that was all about; I explained that I had spent more money on Kevin's education than Valerie's so I felt I wanted to even the score. My daughter-in-law, Sarah always says "life isn't fair," but I try to even the score if possible.

Valerie went to Wisconsin Rapids to the technical college for child care. She wanted to stay in Rapids, but I didn't think the expense or hassle would be worth it. Once she and I talked about it she decided living at home would work just fine. We had a phone line installed upstairs that was both her phone line and the computer line; we were still on dial-up for the internet which was our only option in the country. I felt the child care program was expensive with lots of busy work. The program was to help individuals interested in daycare to get a business started. There was one business class that was necessary and most helpful. In that class, she learned about all the paperwork involved when dealing with state programs and taking care of children. The program was a year-long which meant there were plenty of classes to fill the time; I would call it busy work. I know Valerie would have been right for that area, but the location of her daycare was the issue. She was still living at home, and I didn't feel I wanted a daycare to be in my house. Working for a child care center would not make her much money. It just wasn't meant to be her career. She did gain the poise and confidence while going to Mid-State to apply for a job in Sherry at Kick-a-poo, a cheese packing factory. Raymond found an ad in the paper for positions there, and when she was hired, she never looked back. It was a good fit for her, and she has made many friends while working at that job. She had a five-mile drive one way, and a few times during the summer I would ride to work with her and walk home. Once when Kevin was working in Plover, during the summer before his senior year in high school, I had him drop me off 15 miles from home to walk back home. I was working on a hiking program, so when a 15-mile hike was required, I walked along highway 10 in the early morning. That is what I did for exercise. People have asked Raymond if he can't find something for me to do on the farm for activity. He could, but I was not interested.

Kevin did work one summer at Kick-a-poo, but Val and Kevin didn't ride together to work. Valerie would work extra hours if asked and Kevin wanted to put in his eight hours and get home. Not to sit, he enjoyed roller-blading down County Road S in the afternoon heat. I prefer my form of exercise. I tried that roller-blading sport, and I wasn't comfortable going down a hill at breakneck speeds. On blacktop, it doesn't have to be much of a hill when in a car, and a person can really pick up speed on the smooth surface. While he was working in Sherry, he once wanted to get out of work on a Friday because he wanted to be with his friends from SPASH one last time. He wanted me to call in sick for him. I explained he had already been with them for the last time, so he headed off to work.

Kevin only applied to the University of Wisconsin-Madison because that was the only place he wanted to attend. As other students in his class were getting acceptance letters from other colleges, I was getting concerned. I finally got him to start another application, but it was never completed and sent because his acceptance letter came from Madison. Some of his friends applied to the University of Wisconsin-Stevens Point which was easier to get into than Madison, but they used that school as their back-up in case their first choice didn't work. He was determined to go to Madison. Also, he had to go with a roommate; he was not willing to get just anyone when he went to Madison. Thus he tried to talk Mark Blenker and Jeff Wight into going with him. As it turned out, Jeff was his roommate for the first three years. For their first two years, they lived in Chadborne, a dorm that was just remodeled. The room didn't look much different than the dorm where I lived my first year in college. A small room is a small room, but they did have to make some changes to the wiring because these kids were coming with computers. When the boys were assigned a time to move into the dorm, that first year we had to try to get to the campus when about ten others from SPASH were going to arrive. The purpose of the timing was so all of them could go together to get their football tickets because they wanted to sit together in a SPASH section; which was easy to find because you just looked for the section where everyone is wearing red, and they are all standing. FYI: when attending a football game in Madison everyone is in red, and there is no need for the bleachers because no one sits to watch the game.

Kevin started college with six college credits because of the Economics program at SPASH. Mr. McCaffrey taught most of those classes. Valerie took Money Management from him, and while she was already a saver, he informed his students of the value of saving money. The classes Kevin took offered Advancement Placement credit if you passed a test. These were micro and macroeconomics classes that gave students the opportunity to study the production, distribution, and use of goods and services. Students now days can start college with enough credits to skip one or two semesters thus saving money for their parents. Kevin could have also gotten a scholarship if he had worked harder filling out the forms. He explained he felt all was good because he already had the "Connie Milz" scholarship. I informed him that some teachers I worked with thought I didn't owe my children a college degree. "Don't listen to those teachers," was his answer.

During the summers our children helped on the farm. Valerie was never a complainer, but then Raymond worked around our schedules before he planned on the three of us contributing our efforts to the cause. Once when Kevin had plans to play ball with some boys, he was asked if he could stay on the farm to unload hay because we needed the wagons for the next day to do the baling. He didn't complain and explained to me that he would be building muscle tossing the bales around and getting a tan at the same time. My little boy was growing up and maturing.

Before Kevin left for college, we celebrated our 25th wedding anniversary in July 1995. The kids planned three events for us; Mass at St. Wenceslaus, donut social after the Mass, and lunch at Hamm's. Valerie sent invitations to family and friends that would not see the announcement in the church bulletin. We explained that we were requesting their presence but no presents. I thought that if we didn't get presents there would be no need for thank you notes. Kevin got the donuts from Stevens Point for the social. He picked them up because he had stayed in Point the night before at a friend's home. He arrived in Milladore just about the time Mass was going to start, and I asked him where the donuts were; in the car and he would get them downstairs after Mass. No, I explained to him, they had to be down there now. Kevin could be dependable but not early. Everything worked out so nice, and I felt I needed to write notes to people thank them for taking the time to attend. We have two pictures of that day because Francis Cherney had a camera. If he had not been there, we would have nothing for posterity. We are blessed with good neighbors in Milladore. During the event at Hamm's, I had our wedding pictures on display with a copy of the sermon that Father Barnabas, my cousin Jerry McDonald preached at our wedding. Father Jerry, didn't live long enough to celebrate our 25th anniversary but he would check with me at family celebrations to see if we were still married. I noticed our parish priest Father John Wisneski taking the time to read his sermon.

Raymond mentioned how cold and miserable the winter of 1996 was in Wisconsin. There was a day that the weather was so bad the stock market closed as well as SPASH. Once my kids were out of SPASH, I didn't pay attention to what was going on in Point. The school was closed a few days in a row, the only reason I know this is because Sarah told me that she remembers they had so many days to make up that Senior Skip day was canceled. School officials said seniors would not go through their graduation ceremony if they missed on the Skip day. It was Sarah's last year in high school, and this "straight A student" had been waiting her entire academic career for this skip day only to have it ripped away from her. Isn't it funny how we can remember things that happened years ago?

Raymond was fifty years old in January 1997, and we had a party for him to celebrate. Again, Hamm's, in Milladore was the perfect place to have our gathering. Duane Hamm would allow us to bring in the food and I just had him serve the drinks. Bernie Wahl, a teacher from Marshfield, told me what he was doing for his wife's fifty-year celebration; he gave her 50 things of 50 items. He started with 50 pennies, then 50 nickels, and continued that up to dollars; gets costly if you move beyond the dollar bill. I just copied his idea and came up with a few more of my own, like another forty-three items. I tried to make the 50 things consumable, so we didn't have to dust anything. A 50-ounce container of liquid laundry would work. Another one of my ideas was 50 promises. Three examples are: Valerie would wash Ray's truck on the weekend, Kevin promised to milk on the second Tuesday of every week was his idea, and I promised a kiss every day of the week. The project turned out to be time-consuming, but there are 24 hours in a day, so we did get it completed. We didn't wrap all the items or take them to Hamm's for the party. This was not repeated when he turned sixty; ten more items would have broken me.

I moved back to Senior High to teach in September 1994. The reason for the move was because of a need for another Physical Education teacher at the high school. The 9th graders had been moved from Junior High and became part of the senior high. Kevin mentioned at the time that he would be angry if he were a 9th grader in Marshfield at the time of the move. He didn't explain his comment, and I didn't think about it until the Class of 1998 were seniors. In my experience seniors are a mature class ready to go out in the world or on to college. That class was different in that they seemed more like a set of juniors who needed another year in school to become more serious about the future. Thinking back to what Kevin said, I realized this class never got to be "top dog" when they were in Junior High. This was the first year of being the oldest and wisest, in school and they had a hard time. It would have been good if they could have experienced that as 9th graders three years earlier. Life is interesting.

There are things I will miss from this time when my kids were growing up. Have you ever thought about the last time you will be doing an activity? Like the last time your child will be leaving home to get on a school bus, or the last 4-H meeting. I want to write about some of my "last experiences" but the last time doesn't stand out, but I remember all of them as an experience that I will miss.

I didn't take a picture of two Point school buses in my yard at one time. When my kids rode the bus home at night, their buses would meet someplace after leaving Junior and Senior High to combine kids from the buses into family groups; then both the buses didn't have to stop at every family's home. I don't understand bus routes, but there are people that can figure out the best route which makes for the least number of miles traveled. If when these buses were meeting one of them were late, the exchange might not happen. This was the reason I saw two buses in our yard at the same time. I didn't have a camera handy, so it is only a memory; I had one chance to get a picture, because that didn't happen again, and I missed it.

Before he could drive, Kevin came up with the idea that when he was going to senior high if I took him to the other side of Milladore in the morning to meet the bus he had an extra twenty-five minutes at home. At that time the bus was coming out of Milladore heading west to our place, once he was on, they headed further to the west on the country roads before going back to town to pick up kids in town. After leaving town, the bus headed east to Trestik road to go south and then return to Highway 10; we waited for it to return to 10 and he got on at the stop sign. This did give him time to finish his breakfast, and I just headed to school. This turned out to be a good deal for both of us.

During Kevin's last year in SPASH, we would have breakfast on Wednesday mornings before he drove to school and I headed to work. We always had the same order, and it was ready for us when we arrived which must have been about 7 am. Not sure of her last name but Sally was the waitress's first name. There were no dishes, and we had plenty of time to eat. All four of us couldn't do that because Valerie started work by 6 am, and Raymond began milking cows even earlier. One Wednesday we both forgot it was our day to eat breakfast out so when Raymond went to Hamm's for breakfast, Sally asked what happened to us. He didn't know, but he did pay for our meals that had been made and tossed. I am sure I paid him back, so no one has to worry about him. Not sure when our last breakfast was, but I know we didn't continue into the summer because of Kevin's summer job. He had to earn some money for college.

Our last 4-H meeting was just before the Marshfield Fair in 1991 which is held on Labor Day weekend. Valerie didn't feel she would have time for 4-H once she started at Mid-State in the fall. Because his sister wasn't going to continue,

Kevin decided to quit at the same time. North County Line was the name of their club which is still active in our area. When they were in 4-H, I was also very involved, which provided my social life. I remember when Kevin played his last basketball game at SPASH, one of the mothers asked what we were going to do for entertainment next year without basketball. I don't remember her name, but I am sure I never saw her again. Life moves on, and we can always find something to do.

Is there something in your life that you had done for so long that you can't remember when it started? For Ray and me our breakfast club would be a great example. There are six of us that go to 8 am Mass on Sunday morning and meet for breakfast in Junction City. My brain is a storage shed, I'll find what I need in time, so let me start searching. I know we would go to Mass on Sunday morning when Kevin and Valerie were still home, but when they went to breakfast with us, they wanted to eat and leave. Ray and I enjoyed visiting with others that also were at breakfast at Hamm's in Milladore. Again, Hamm's was the local pub where we had gathered for many family functions. In time because the kids were not going with us we were joined by Karen and Dick Cherney who also would end up there after Mass. I'm not sure when Sue and Ray Linzmeier joined us but I think it was before Hamm's closed and we had to go to Junction City for our "breakfast club." Valerie hasn't been out of high school for thirty years but it is getting close to thirty, so I believe our breakfast club has been meeting for just over thirty years. Lots of world problems have been discussed, and I think we could solve a few if one of our group would run for President. No more on that subject except to say I don't tolerate missing the breakfast club on Sunday mornings. My week doesn't get off to a good start without input from the members of this breakfast club.

Before moving on to the next chapter, I want to say a few more things about higher education and what it will do for you. Every individual doesn't need a degree to follow their dreams. I encouraged my kids to decide what they enjoy doing and see if there is a career in that area. Both of my kids developed an excellent work ethic and are contributing members of society. All parents want that for their children if they are good role models themselves.

One Christmas I purchased sweatshirts for Valerie and Kevin that said; "Dear Santa, I want it all." I would be willing to bet that they were on sale when I purchased them because if you think about the saying, it isn't the best idea to teach your kids. But never pass up a "teachable" moment. We discussed what a person needs to do if they want it all. Go to school, get an education, get a good job, and buy it all, which is easy enough if you are pushed by your dreams and not by your problems. One more thought is the idea of being happy with what you have and not being concerned about what you don't have.

Where is Raymond in all of this? Raymond milked those cows every day through the years our kids went to school and started in the world of work. They knew what that world of work was all about because Raymond demonstrated it all the time to them. You know what they say about dairy farmers; "they do it twice a day." Actually, some dairy farmers milk their cows three times a day, but Raymond never tried that idea.

CHAPTER TEN

"The secret of getting ahead is getting started."
Mark Twain

At one point in 1998, I was depressed; it took me a while to figure out what the issue was, but finally realized my two children were going to be leaving home. It wasn't like they were married and gone because neither Valerie nor Kevin were even engaged. At the time, I knew what was coming because I could "see the writing on the wall." During the years of my teaching CCD, I would advise students to turn to God when they had a problem in their life where help is needed. After seeing a note in the church bulletin that was asking people to join the daily rosary, I had my answer. For years I had seen two or more cars in the parking lot every morning as I rushed by to get someplace. I joined the group of six people on Monday, June 15, 1998, at 6:30 am. They were Leonard and Dawn Haasl, Bob and Audrey Heitzinger, and Pete and Annette Beaver. When they said, "daily" they meant every day of the week including Sunday. It didn't take long for my depression to pass, and I was no longer concerned with the empty nest that was in my future. I learned what "this too shall pass," really means. Stop worrying about the future because worry is just the lack of faith in God. Now twenty years later I am still saying the rosary with the four that remain. First Dawn went to her heavenly reward and a few years later her husband, Leonard joined her. In the years since I joined there were times, I missed during the week when my hours at the bank changed, and I could not say the rosary at church and make it to work on time. During those years I joined them on the weekends. We had changed the time to 6:55 am, and I could not move fast enough in the morning except on the weekends. The reason for that time change was to encourage others to join. Our daily Mass at St Wenceslaus is at 7:20 am, and people could come a few minutes early to say the rosary and then stay for Mass. It worked because at times there are a few more people that joined us.

As I say the rosary I try to make every prayer count; the Apostle's Creed at the beginning is said for my parish priest as well as those who were my priests in the past. The first Our Father I offer to God for the one person here on earth that needs it most, the Lord knows the name of that person. The three Hail Mary's are said for my students from the past. I hope I helped them in some way during their life. When I say a decade of the rosary, I have a specific person for each of the five mysteries. The first mystery is said for Raymond as well as his family and friends. That would include me and just about everyone else we know. The second is said for Valerie in the same manner; for her friends and family. The third is for Kevin, Sarah, Andrew, and Parker; fourth is for those needing extra prayers because they are dealing with cancer or something or might be close to death. I ask the Lord to include those family and friends that He knows are in need of an extra prayer. The final mystery is said for those who have died and are no longer with us on earth except in our heart.

Now it was time for me to think about what I would be doing when I would retire in 2003 from teaching. I have always been a planner, and I like to make a "to do" list when I have a lot to completed in the next few days. The thing I like about a well written "to do" list is the checking off or crossing out of items or tasks on the list as they are completed. At the end of the day when I am tired at least

I have something to show for the day. The secret to writing that list is not to say "clean the basement," but break the task down into manageable steps. If it takes too much time to write the steps, then go to a "20-minute" project to complete the larger task. Let me explain. Everyone has 20 extra minutes in a day, so work on the large project of cleaning the basement for 20 minutes per day. Use a stopwatch and only work for 20 minutes. It works because my basement is clean and stays clean because Raymond works on it once a year whether it needs it or not. Another way I did clean my basement was to use Craigslist.com. Have you ever wanted to sell something or just get rid of an item you no longer need? Craigslist.com is the answer. The first thing I put on was Kevin's bed, and I listed it for free. The first person to call was on their way, and about 3 hours after posting on the site it was gone. When I was ready to clear out my basement, I posted a filing cabinet for free, and the first call was a woman interested in the dining room buffet that was in the background. I went back to the picture I had posted, and that buffet did look good. The story was that her Grandmother had one just like it but her older sister had it. I told her she could come to look at it because I was willing to give it to her for free. Have you ever noticed that when you take something to the basement, you no longer need it? That is what I had in my basement, many items I had no use for, and I was willing to part with everything if someone was willing to move the stuff out of the basement. When that woman came, I told her my story, everything you see is free. When she came back with two guys and two pickup trucks the only things I had left in my basement was a set of shelves and a freezer. A perfect way to clean out a basement; and I have learned to "let go of things." With a clutter-free basement, you might think my entire home is like that but, that is a work in progress.

My plans for the future were to retire from teaching in June of 2003 and find another career. Wendy Jones, a friend that I taught with when I was at the elementary level, said I needed to decide if I wanted a career or a job. After considering all the pros and cons I decided on a career, but not what career. While I was still teaching, I started with a few ideas. The first one was purchasing a house in Milladore, which I planned to remodel and open as a bed-and-breakfast.

Hindsight shows that was my dumbest idea, but it was a project that ended well. I didn't spend that much to purchase it, but then I started the remodel which took plenty of money. I only worked on the house when I had the money up front, and I had a few renters which meant there was someone watching the place. Long story short, I saw the error of my ways, but now Valerie lives in that home only a mile from me; it is nice to have one child living close to me.

Next idea was working for Artistic Impressions as an art broker. The company didn't want you to say you were having a party to sell art but an art show to display the art and we were the people in the middle, the brokers. My final thought about that idea was it was just an expensive "Tupperware" party, and I purchased lots of the art with the commission I made. Bottom line is I needed a job to support that job, but it was fun.

Moving on, I saw an ad in the paper by IntoEdVentures where they were looking for people to place foreign exchange students. I called and talked to the woman, Carla Kuehl, and it sounded like something I might like to do. I walked out of my office after talking to her and told the first student I saw what I was going to be doing. She explained that her family wanted to host a student for the next school year. I was hooked, how easy was that to place my first student? I need to explain that was the only student I placed with one contact. If you placed a student after ten contacts or phone calls, you considered that a positive day's work with an excellent outcome. But working for that company was very enjoyable, and we traveled to several other countries in Europe because I received those trips after I had placed at least seven or more students. Only once did I place enough students to earn three free trips but that was a lot of work during the school year. If you have a perfect placement, you visit the student and host family every semester and write a report. If the placement is less than perfect, you might be visiting every month and even move the student to another host family. All of that experience made life interesting.

Before the dust settled, I even considered opening a restaurant in Milladore. If you know me this was by far the worst idea because I don't enjoy cooking or baking all that much. Plus I am always on a "see food" diet; I see food, and I eat it. This would not have been good for my waistline or hips; they say, "a moment on the lips and a lifetime on the hips." I am not sure I have that quote right, but it does seem like it could happen.

As it turned out, I wanted both of my children to have completed their schooling after high school, and then once they were engaged, I knew it would be more comfortable paying for the weddings while I was still teaching. Valerie was married in 2000 and Kevin was married in 2002. We will come back to those events; I want to explain what I did to welcome in the year 2000.

In the Sunday paper on July 10, 1994, I found the following notice. "By the way, Monday (July 11, 1994) marks '2000 Days Before 2000,' and idea trademarked by Chicago artist Adrienne Sioux Koopersmith, 41. She says that if you take a moment each day from July 11, 1994, to December 31, 1999, to do something you ordinarily wouldn't do-like start a hobby, volunteer, or eat a chocolate chip cookie-you'll gain so much. (If you pick cookies, though, we're talking weight gain.)" This gave me the idea to write 2000 letters. On Wednesdays, I would write to my parents, and on Thursdays, I wrote Ray's mother. Those two letters were often the same. I completed that project which gave me a volume of paper to deal with because I kept a copy of each letter written. I am not talking a handwritten letter, but I used the computer to cut and paste some sections. I numbered every letter; #1 was written to Raymond, #2 to Valerie, and #3 to Kevin. I don't remember what Ray or Valerie said, but Kevin said I was nuts. That would be his opinion, not necessarily fact.

As my "2000 letters" project was coming to an end, we were also dealing with the Y2K impending disaster. If you are too young to remember or have forgotten, Y2K was the issue of our computers no being able to handle the year 2000. The possible disaster would be that as we would ring in the New Year, our computers would crash because their programs only went to December 31, 1999. I found an article written by the American Red Cross explaining to people how they should prepare for Y2K. There were five suggestions:

1) have plenty of extra batteries for flashlights

2) have extra cash because banks would not be able to process checks
3) have extra food and medications in case the supply chain was broken
4) have vehicles filled with gas
5) have a battery operated radio.

Our family only had an issue with our Discover credit card. When a new one was issued with an expiration date in the next century, it would get rejected. We would use another card and decided we didn't need Discover, so that is a credit card of the past. I am sure businesses needed to get new machines, and all was right with the world. The next big debate was when the new century started; January 1, 2000, or January 1, 2001.

In 1988 Raymond stopped raising his calves because he found someone that would do it for him. The bull calves were never kept on the farm and usually went out within a week of being born. Now the same was true of the heifer calves. If they were here more than a week the kids, especially Kevin wanted to know when they were going out because they feed them at night. One calf to feed wasn't a big issue but when there were two or more it was time to get them shipped. When Ray's heifers were raised by another person, Ray had the first opportunity to repurchase them as springing heifers. It was a good deal for him because as the kids were getting closer to graduation from high school they were getting busier with school activities. He was preparing for a day when both of his children would be gone, and all the work would fall on him.

In the summer of 1998, I took a class to learn more about using a computer. After I had my Masters Degree, I didn't have to stay with my original field of study. It was time to improve my skills with the newest technology. Our IT director at the high school at the time, Dean Marquart said that any teacher that learned to use a computer would be making their life easier. I taught Physical Education, I didn't believe him, but I did want to know what all the "brew ha ha" (is that even a word?) was about so I joined STAT; Summer Technology Academy for Teaching that summer. Another "long story short," Dean was right, and I guess it wasn't a big surprise to me. My "2000 letters" project was completed only because I was using a computer. We learned so many ways to organize our life and make things easier to stay on task; it was a very productive summer. I would never want to give up my computer but let it be said that the first one I purchased most likely was not used to its full capacity. I know the one I have now can do more than I use it for in my daily life. Test my idea or thought; sit next to a ten-year-old while they are using a computer.

For me, I was still enjoying my teaching career, but I knew I should retire because I didn't want to be that teacher that didn't want to try new ideas. I wanted to try a new career but didn't know what direction to go. I had started my career at the high school, remaining there for twelve years. When an opportunity presented itself to move to the elementary level, I tried that for twelve years. In September of 1994, I moved back to the high school to a new office and remained there for nine years. Columbine happened April 20, 1999, when I was at the high school. After that incident, I remember talking to other teachers about any student you had just disciplined. Was that the next one to bring a gun to school to even a score? We all spent some time second-guessing ourselves. Then there was 911; September 11, 2001. I was in the weight room ready to start my second class of the day. The first student entering the weight room said I should turn on the radio to hear what happened in New York. The Twin Towers had been attacked. The radio was on, and as we looked at each other we heard the news; information was being shared as we listened. I can only imagine what teachers in New York were dealing with because I am sure they had students in their class that would have been working at the Towers. Where were you when the Towers were attacked?

Before I was going to retire, we knew there was going to be two weddings in the family. Valerie was married April 29, 2000, and at the time Kevin and Sarah might have been engaged. Valerie's future mother-in-law, Thea took care of all the flowers for the wedding. She had been working as a florist for many years, and because of her experience and talent, she did a fantastic job. I suggested we go with artificial flowers because they look so real, and would be easy to deal with on the day of the wedding. However, because of Thea's career, she wanted to go with real. At one point she realized for this wedding she would have lots to do on the day of the wedding as the mother of the groom, so we settled on artificial. Those flowers cost a total of fifty dollars, a reasonable price for the year 2000 and they were beautiful.

Valerie's shower was at St Wenceslaus parish basement. I had the invitations printed because I was helping my sisters get the event ready. Those invitations were proofed by more than just me but when I picked them up at the printer's the misspelled word jumped off the page at me. The first "s" in Wenceslaus was missing. Valerie was so easy to please; she was not concerned; even if she is the best speller in our family.

Father Berg was not our parish priest at the time, but he married Valerie because Father John was on a fishing vacation. Father John talked to me about the fact that his vacation was already planned and he was concerned that I would be upset. It wasn't my wedding, and again Valerie knew and liked Father Berg. It worked out nice to have him back in our parish for a day; he was the parish priest when Ray and I came to Milladore. Just before the ceremony, Sarah was sitting with Nicole Youngblood, the flower girl and they were discussing her pretty bouquet. Nicole was sad because she wasn't going to get to keep her beautiful flowers that came from Valerie. Sarah explained that they were her flowers to keep and she didn't need to give them back to the bride. Then Sarah asked Nicole what grade she was in school? "Third grade," was her answer. I was just sitting taking a moment to relax when I heard the answer. "You are not, you are in Kindergarten," was my explanation. Nicole was just messing with Sarah, what a kid!

The gift opening was in Milladore at Valerie's home which gave her an opportunity to show everyone where they would be living. It was a beautiful day, so we opened the gifts on the front lawn, and walked them into the house to be put away later. When they were opening the cards, they found one from some people they didn't know. We do think it was in the card box from the last wedding. So that card was returned with the box.

Sad to say, today Valerie is divorced. Her ex-husband wanted to move back to Wisconsin Rapids because he didn't like living rent free in Milladore. It is best to leave the topic alone and move on to happier days. All is right with the world, and Valerie is happy.

For Kevin and Sarah's wedding, she used a florist that was close to the family home in Stevens Point, Field of Flowers. Sarah's favorite flowers were tulips at the time and the owner, Sandy Obremski explained that they would be difficult to keep them looking good for the day. I know the flowers used for the altar were artificial because we just rented them and Sandy would take them back after the ceremony. The thing I remember most about meeting with Sandy was every time Sarah asked for her opinion; Sandy would say, "What do you like, it is your wedding." I know I heard it said about five times during that meeting, because later when we were looking for a photographer, Sarah said it back to me, "It is my wedding." Fun times, while planning a wedding.

Their wedding shower was at RiverEdge. The cost of the meal wasn't too bad until Ray's sisters and sister-in-laws bellied up to the bar. It was getting late in the day, and we were sure it was close enough to 5 pm so no one would judge us. Not that it would have stopped that crew; we were celebrating. The rehearsal dinner was at the same place, and when Jeff Wight arrived at our house to attend that event, he was disappointed that I didn't have a big sign announcing the wedding. Guess he missed the silhouette couple standing in the yard dressed in wedding finery. He felt I needed something more significant; I told him to wait until the next day. I had a twenty-foot green cow at the end of the driveway that people saw as they made their way from the ceremony to the reception. The day after the wedding Sarah's family were told that the cow was marking the farm where the gift opening was to take place. On Sunday I had pulled the green cow onto the front lawn. A few of Sarah's relatives realized they missed our farm when they arrived at the church; the cow was hard to see from the road. But back to the rehearsal dinner; Sarah's mom, Nancy came up with a beautiful idea for the evening. People were asked to bring something to put into a box that would be closed and wrapped for Kevin and Sarah's 25th wedding anniversary. I remember Sarah's Grandmother put an angel in because she felt she would be an angel in heaven looking down on the couple in 2027 when it was time to open it. She was right. My sister Patricia put a bottle of wine in for them to use to celebrate. Kevin's God-parents, Butch and Karen Milz put 100 dollar bill in the box. Me? I do not know what I put in the box but I hope I did put something neat or creative in there, I don't remember.

So with both of my children finished with higher education, married, and on their own, I was ready to consider a second career. Wendy Jones, a friend that I taught with for twelve years, talked about the difference between a job and a career. I didn't want a job; I wanted something that I could work at and still learn something. Also, I did not want a career that needed more education than I already had on my resume. Before I submitted my resignation, I had a job teaching at the University of Wisconsin-Stevens Point for the fall semester of 2003 and the spring of 2004. There were two classes for me to teach which I had taken during my tenure as a Physical Education student. My master's degree qualified me for the position which was as an adjunct professor. If you look up "adjunct" you will find the definition as, "something added to the main thing, less important and not needed, but helpful." July 14, 2003, I started a journal about my career at the University. The second and last entry was August 18, 2003. I wish I had written more about that year. What I remember learning from that job was that I was pleased to have taught in the public school system K-12. I would never have taught at the university for thirty-three years because students at the college level expected an A, even when they did not complete the work as required. It was necessary to make the requirements very clear or you would be challenged at every turn. It was an exciting year, and I was pleased to have the opportunity, but I would not bother to complete a doctoral degree which would have been necessary to continue at the University.

In the fall of 2004, because I was not going back to the university, I worked with Manpower which offered a battery of tests to see what I would be suited to do. I was looking for a part-time job and was told I might have better luck if I go full-time. Manpower found me a job at Associated Bank in Stevens Point. The building the bank was in was the old library in Point. I had taken my children there for story hour and many other summer activities when they were in grade school. I was hired for a month to replace the receptionist that took a month off because of family issues. I met some of the most helpful people and enjoyed the job so much I didn't look forward to quitting, so when my boss, Karen Sidoff told me about a position they had open as a part-time teller I applied and was hired. What I did was clean out a storage room, it was my way of making myself indispensable. During my downtime, I would clean shelves and cubby holes and put "like things" together. When someone decided they needed to order new bank envelopes with a printed return address, I just showed them where our stash was in the storage room. People would order things like yellow markers and stuff them someplace; never use the markers again because no one knew where they were located. I put everything in a central location and because the person that did the ordering was me when markers were needed I knew where they could be located.

After about a year of working at Associated I realized my health insurance was not going to last until we were eligible for Medicare; thus I had to apply for full time to receive benefits. I was working from 8 to 5 with an hour lunch. Those were some long days, and it took a few weeks to get into a pattern. There is something to be said for the difference of a corporate bank vs. a small community bank. Raymond and I had been with Advantage Community Bank since the days when the farm carried a debt. We remained with that bank because we liked the service and we had a credit line that gave us flexibility when funding new projects or activities on the farm. I didn't like the way people were treated at a corporate bank, but I could not change the rules if you overdraw your account by two dollars or two thousand dollars the fine is over thirty dollars. I also learned that many people don't know how to handle money. You can't spend the entire paycheck; some of every check needs to be saved. You have to work for your money, but you need to save some money to work for you unless you want to work for the rest of your life. To retire you need to have some money saved. Also in the larger bank, I found that even with my skills it was difficult to advance my position beyond the teller. My son explained to me that it was my age, but that is never mentioned. In the fall of 2006, Ray and I meet for lunch with Chris Myhre, the CEO/President of Advantage Community Bank to sign some papers for our line of credit. Mr. Myhre mentioned the purpose of the line was to borrow money which we didn't have to, but it was nice to have if necessary. When Chris realized I had been working for another bank for almost two years, he told I should work for him because now I was trained and I could move up faster in a smaller community bank. Long story, short; that was the best move I could have made. I was hired part-time for more money, and in less than six months I was able to go full-time. Because I didn't use the health insurance at first, the bank paid my a stipend each month. After about a year I was hired as the manager of the Mosinee branch which was a position I held for almost ten years. I was pleased with my move not that resigning from Associated was easy; I had enjoyed the individuals at that bank. I just had to get started at another bank to develop in my new career, thus the secret of getting ahead. The lesson I learned was that I again was working with some wonderful people that are very professional.

CHAPTER ELEVEN

"Life is a story, make yours a best seller."
Unknown

Before I retired from teaching, I had the opportunity to teach one class at the Junior High. I say "opportunity" because I wanted to think of it as a positive experience. It has been said that junior high teachers are either saints or crazy and in my opinion, I am neither, so I looked at the opportunity to teacher there as a new experience. It was fun, it was the last class of the day, and I was able to walk from senior high, so it was a built-in opportunity to get some exercise. The reason it was me that got to teach there was because I was the department head at the time and I had to select the person from senior high that went to the junior high. Instead of telling someone else to go, I just went myself. Gerry DeSmet was a Physical Education teacher at the Junior High while I was teaching in Marshfield. One afternoon when he returned from lunch he told me that his grandchildren were so much fun that he should have had them first. Now that I have my own grandchildren I know what he was trying to say because we can't do it in that order in the real world. I have a magnet on my refrigerator that says, "Grandchildren are your reward for not killing your children." The reason I have that magnet was that my son, their father, pointed it out to me once while we were shopping together. When Andrew and Parker saw it, they were confused and acted a bit disappointed with me. Someday, I hope they will understand that thought and maybe even understand the humor.

In July of 2014, I found a book, My Quotable Kid; A Parent's Journal of Unforgettable Quotes designed by Grace Partridge. I know I did not purchase it from Amazon, but I was able to find it on that site if anyone wants a copy. The reason I bought it was to record quotes from my grandchildren, Andrew Matthew Milz and Parker Thomas Milz. The quotes in that book are not just from my grandchildren but my two children as well as other family and friends. The first quote was Valerie's "I hate you" statement from chapter five of this book. John Hollar's statement about how to teach children needed to be in this book. "Tell them how to do it, show them how to do it, and then do it yourself." May I use the term, priceless? The pages are not numbered but I know I have not made it a quarter of the way through that book. I'll get it done someday. "Sitting" is the issue I fight, if I sit too long, I find it hard to get up and get moving again. I have heard that sitting too much is as bad as smoking.

Another journal that I have started is titled "Andrew and Parker Stories." My sister Nancy won the journal while we were on a Longaberger bus trip. Do you know what Longaberger baskets are? When I was working at Advantage Community Bank in Mosinee, I remember one young teller trying to explain to a woman about my age why she, the teller, was willing to pay so much for a Coach purse. I feel that the Coach purse is an over-priced purse. I told the gal it is like a Longaberger basket, over-priced. She collected Longaberger baskets so then she understood the Coach purse concept. The first five pages of the journal explain how the Longaberger Company was started and after I added three pages with notes and pictures of our trip I needed to do something with the book. Stories and pictures about my Grandkids was the perfect solution to complete the book. I am well over half done with that book, yet another work in progress. On the front of the book is a picture of the boys when Andrew is just over two years, and Parker is about six months old. Sarah wanted to take a picture of her boys, but Andrew wanted just his picture taken, thus the reason Andrew has his hand over Parker's eyes.

Another set of books that I started were given to me by the boys for my birthday in 2010. The name is All About Grandma & Me; The Story of Us-to write together written by Mandy Jordan. I searched Amazon, and you can find just about anything you want on that site, which might have been where Sarah got them. Those two books are just about finished, and I want to give them to the boys for Christmas of some year. As implied in the title the boys and I are supposed to work on it together, but we live over 900 miles apart which doesn't help. When I visit, I have a few pages in mind to complete, and I will get it done sometime soon. It is always good to have projects to work on, so a person doesn't get bored. These two books are the closest to being completed, so there is hope for me to get them done soon. I have heard that "being idle eats at your soul." I do not know who said that, I would give the person credit if I knew, but I wrote it down when I found it because I believe it to be true.

When I do get those books listed above completed, I plan to give them to the boys, but I will not send them in the mail. The first week in January of 2016 we all went on a Disney cruise. I worked on scrapbooks for the boys while on that trip, I wrote stories about our experience, and added the pictures I took. When they were visiting in the summer of 2016, I asked them questions about the trip and recorded their answers. I felt that it would be a neat surprise to receive the books in the mail once they were home. You know that tracking number the US postal service gives you? That will tell you the last place your package was scanned, but it doesn't help to locate the package. The boys never received the books, and nothing was returned to me. Insurance? That is just money which means very little compared to what those items were worth. Now when mailing something; I try just to smile and nod when the person hands me the tracking number. They point out that I can take a survey, but they already know they lose things, why do I have to tell them?

What makes my life a best seller is the next generation and the notes I have about our time together. Toward the end of the summer of 2012, when the boys were still living in Kingsport, Tennessee Sarah wrote a note that said, "Definitely ready for first grade next week." Why? As the story goes, Andrew told Sarah that Parker was going to hit him. When Sarah checked with Parker, he explained that was true because "Andrew is looking at me." Andrew was six years old while Parker was four at the time of the encounter. Sarah always gets a picture of the first day of school. The year Andrew started kindergarten his smile could not have been bigger, but that wasn't the best part about the picture; it was the sad little brother sitting, not facing the camera because Andrew was getting to go to school and he had to stay home.

We have been fortunate that Sarah has been willing to travel to Wisconsin during July with her boys to stay at her parents' cottage. Someone asked her how that is possible with her job. She explained, "I take my work with me." While she is a registered nurse, she doesn't work out of the home so with all that knowledge she keeps her family healthy. Kevin usually flies in, using a one-way ticket and stays for a week to visit and then drives home with his family.

In July of 2014, Sarah and I took the boys to the Madison State Capitol for a tour of the building. Andrew was telling Parker how laws were made by the senators and legislators. His knowledge about the activity came from his time in school; he was eight at the time. Parker must have been listening to his older brother as he was sharing his knowledge of the legislative process. The reason I say this is because later in the day when Parker came out of the restroom room, we heard him say, "Hey Andrew I saw one of those guys." Following him out of the restroom was a distinguished looking gentleman dressed in a suit. Parker knew he had spotted one of those guys that make laws at the capitol we were visiting.

When Kevin came to visit Wisconsin that July he overheard the following conversation between his two boys;

Andrew: "Parker, do you know everything?"

Parker: "No."

Andrew: "You are lucky you said 'no,' I was ready to ask you some really hard questions."

As a side note to the above interaction, I am sure Andrew could ask me some hard questions that I would not have an answer to, especially if those questions had to do with computers. He helped me set up a website with my Google account, and the questions were endless; do want this or that? I had no answers; I needed to think about it. Kids and computers are a mystery to me. I do try to keep up because I know computers have made my life both more interesting and more manageable. As an example, once when I was checking to see if my beneficiary information is up-to-date on an account, we found that Valerie's last name was wrong because since her divorce she went back to using Milz. Upon checking Kevin's address was wrong, so there was much to be updated. The necessary forms were e-mailed to me, and I scanned the signed copies back to her. That was fast and easy because of our computers. Are all your accounts updated with beneficiary information? There is no time like the present to check.

Raymond and I celebrated our forty-fifth wedding anniversary on July 25th, 2015 when Kevin's family was visiting Wisconsin. They took us out to eat in Shawano and while we were waiting for our meal I told Parker that when the waitress came back, I would ask that the children's meals be served before the adults' meals. The night before when we ate out it happened in reverse, the adults had their meals before our boys and that doesn't work just right. Parker said, "No, Grandma it is your anniversary. You should be first, I am used to waiting." That child is so thoughtful. The next day in church after the Mass the priest asked if anyone was celebrating a birthday or anniversary. Andrew had his hand in the air faster than the speed of light. He always enjoys participating given an opportunity. When he was called on he explained, "My Grandparents have been married for forty-five years. Not these Grandparents, my other Grandparents." The boys were attending church with Nancy and Joe while we were in Milladore that morning. Grandkids are the best.

In September of 2015, Grandma Nancy and I made our way to Signal Mountain to babysit for the boys while Sarah was going to participate in her third Ironman competition. It wears me out just thinking about what that event includes; two-mile swim, 136-mile bike ride, and then a person has a marathon to complete which is 26.2 miles. Kevin was going with her to be a tri-supporter. That title means he would sit, wait, and cheer while Sarah is swimming, biking, and running. While we have gone to see her compete, this time the boys were staying home because they were in school. Before their parents left, the mantra from the boys was, "Don't leave." We have seen Sarah swim in some nasty and windy weather. When this event was postponed because of the weather, and we were returning earlier than planned to Wisconsin, their mantra was, "Don't leave," but now it was directed at us. We love those boys.

Once when I was talking to Grandma Nancy, she said, "We are going to be Grandparents again." Sarah was sitting there, and when I looked at her, she explained to me, "You're not, Becky is expecting." So the other Grandparents have a grandson, Lucas who is living in France. Lucas comes to visit during the summer when the boys are here from Tennessee, so they have the opportunity and becoming good friends. One summer Andrew told me he was going to learn French so he could talk to Lucas. Lucas heard Andrew and said, "My English is very good, so you don't have to do that." Lucas is right; he speaks and understands both English and French. In 2016 when the three cousins were in Wisconsin, we all went to a Timber Rattlers game on July 20, 2016. The game didn't start until 7:07 pm which means we were not staying for the entire game, but it was fun for the five innings we did see. The next day, when Lucas got up, he asked, "Did the Snakes win?" It must have something to do with the translation from English to French.

There is no end to the stories I could include in this chapter about my two Grandchildren, but I need to say Raymond, and I have three Grandsons, while Nancy and Joe have four. The four of us share one Grandson that is in heaven. Carson William Milz lived only a short time here and was taken to heaven to live with Jesus. He died July 20, 2005, just two days before his father was 28 years old. When we lost Carson, Johanna explained to me that Our Lord only takes the best ones to be angels. I must say I was not pleased with the Lord's decision to choose Sarah and Kevin's first born so soon. It did take a few years before I stopped questioning the event; I have resigned to the fact that not all my questions in life have answers. Did you ever hear the story about the Farmer that was asked by a preacher to say grace at a men's breakfast? The farmer got up and said, Lord, I hate lard, buttermilk, and raw white flour. The preacher was concerned about where this was going as the farmer continued, "But Lord when you mix them all together and bake them you get fresh biscuits. So when life gets hard, and we don't understand what you are doing to us, we just have to relax and wait until you are done, and we might get something even better than biscuits." Guess I have to remember that story as my life continues in the future.

Recently when I was visiting Kevin's family, I was thinking about what a wonderful family they are and only then stopped to realize we were able to live through the loss of little Carson. Granma Nancy and I have vowed to live a more pious life so we will be able to make it to heaven to see our first-born Grandson again. I don't want to speak for her, but I am trying to keep that commitment. I received a little blue teddy bear from friends that I was working with at the time. That little bear sits in the back seat of my car and is with me as I travel to remind me of Carson.

With the boys living in Tennessee, I am pleased that I have been able to keep up with their events and lives with Facebook. I know some people are on that site for most of the day; I tend to check it once a day to see if there is anything new that has been posted about Andrew and Parker. At the beginning of the summer in 2016 Sarah posted the following notes about the boys. Andrew had started summer school and came home with an award for "Best Contributor for Discussions." He was ten years old at the time and does always have something to share. I know it is because he likes to read and retains most of what he learns. While the boys were at summer school that day, Sarah must have been going through school papers from the year that was just completed because she posted a journal entry that Parker had written back in September of 2015. His note was, "Seriously; Cinderella is so annoying." As a seven-year-old, he impressed me with the fact that all the words were spelled correctly, but I have no back story about the reason for the comment.

Whenever we are together, there is always more to write because anything either of the boys do, say, or participate in, are considered by me as "genius" and worth written prose. If you are a grandparent, you know exactly what I mean. I know when I am with others talking about my grandchildren as they tell a story it reminds me of another story about my children or grandchildren. I thank God every day for the opportunity I had to be a mother and a grandmother.

So on to the next story. Once when we were on vacation in Florida, we were planning our schedule around watching the Green Bay football game. Kevin mentioned that he didn't enjoy watching football with his wife's family because they were so noisy. Guess he has never had the opportunity to watch a game with my sister Nancy because a person needs ears plugs to not damage your hearing when she is watching Green Bay. But on this Sunday just before the game started, I suggested to the boys that we could get in the pool or hot tub while the rest of the adults were watching the game. Swimsuits were on in less than sixty seconds, and we were out the door. It was a beautiful fall day, and even with the heated pool I preferred the hot tub, but the boys were back and forth. All of a sudden we heard loud screaming and cheering so I sent Andrew to check out what happened. Grandma Nancy informed me that, Brett Farve had just walked onto the field. Guess I can understand what my son was saying about the noise level during a football game. What would it be like now with Aaron Rodgers as our quarterback?

Also, there is no end to the pictures that I can take, print, and put into albums for everyone and anyone to view. It isn't the "in thing" to print pictures because you are supposed to have them digitally stored someplace. This is one of those things that I can't do. I enjoy looking back at photo albums that I have put together over the years. Just as one example, there is the photo Sarah sent of her boys playing the piano. This piano was the one she took lessons on when she was a little girl. Raymond and I picked it up in La Crosse, where her parents were living at the time and took it to Kingsport, Tennessee where they were living at the time. In the picture, Parker is sitting on the bench playing the keys and Andrew is on the floor working the pedals. Andrew was seven years old and taking lessons. I am sure he was explaining to five-year-old Parker what the pedals down below would do as Parker was playing. I had to print that picture, saving it digitally just isn't the same.

Because I print so many pictures, sometimes I find myself with piles of pictures waiting to be put in an album. As I am writing this prose, I have vowed not to print another picture until all the current ones are in albums and labeled. Every once in a while I have to make myself do that or I would not get them done. My objective is always to print pictures and put them in the albums when I get home from picking them up or receiving them in the mail. I do not like to print my pictures because of the cost of the ink. If I spent just fours hours organizing and putting the pictures I have printed I know I could have the task completed and then print more that are being saved on both my phone and camera. Maybe tomorrow is the day it will get done, or I could try the "20-minute" idea defined in chapter six.

My favorite website is Facebook because that is where I see pictures of Andrew and Parker at their events. Sometimes Sarah will post something about the two and what they are up to that day. On September 19, 2017, she said, "My sixth grader just called his fourth-grade brother a 'limiting factor' in his life, and it took a lot not to bust out laughing. The good news is the younger brother wasn't the least bit insulted." There was a comment from Becky Brown Mooney that said, "I am re-evaluating all of the limiting factors in my life." There was no more information about what started this event, but it did make me smile and wonder if I have ever been a limiting to anyone in my life.

December 7, 2015, I received an e-mail from Andrew. He told me the attachment was a "sneak peek" of him playing Good St. Wenceslaus on the piano. The video showed him playing the song which was going to be performed at his upcoming recital. I wrote back, "You are doing a nice job playing the piano, does your Dad play? I paid for him to take piano lessons." Andrew's replay was, "He's the one who taught me jingle bells and not much else." I had to forward that interaction to his father, asking him, "Did you know this?" This was during the day, just after lunch and Kevin is always working hard, so he only had time to reply, "Funny." My only thought is I am glad the money spent on the college degree for Kevin helped him more in his life than those piano lessons.

When a person plays bingo, there is always a number that is your favorite. When I select a bingo card, I look for G56, and I will tell you why. While we were on a Disney cruise some of us went to play bingo while others participated in other activities on the ship. I was in the bingo group with Valerie, Raymond, Parker, Grandpa Joe, and Grandma Nancy. On the ship, they have machines that you can pay for to use and you don't have to do anything except stand up if you only need one more number to win and yell "bingo" when that number is called. I prefer the cards, but Raymond wanted a machine. As we were playing Ray's machine indicated that he needed only one number, but he wanted me to stand up. I told him to give the machine to Parker. When Ray asked him if he wanted Grandpa's machine those little blue eyes were so big. He stood up and was ready for the next number to be called. The only thing we are sure of is that the next number was the number Parker needed, G56. Ray thinks Grandma Nancy yelled bingo before Parker did but I know Parker was letting the room know he had a winning machine. His hands were in the air with a big smile on his face. That money did go to Parker, and I think he is still saving for a boat. He is the one that loves to fish.

Kevin and Sarah's boys are so different. They both joined Boy Scouts at the same time, but Parker only lasted a year. He is more into playing sports. Not basketball, like his father, because when I asked him about that sport, he said, "Grandma, that's a nightmare." Andrew plays the piano, trumpet, and got a guitar from Johanna and Rolf so he might start another instrument. Parker isn't interested in any instruments, which is OK because those boys are each following their own interests.

Of all the names I have been called; and there have been some creative ones, I like Mom and Grandma the best. This is what has made my life a best seller, which all started when I married Raymond.

CHAPTER TWELVE

"Everything will be OK in the end. If it's not OK, it's not the end."
Unknown

It is time to end this book, but the stories have not all been recorded. This book was started in 2016, and the plan was to complete it in 2018 and move on to fiction. After reflecting on my first seventy years, I need to come up with a "to do" list for my next thirty years. While I might have gotten the idea from Tim McGraw, I am not using his lyrics because I never did drink too many beers and I don't regret the twists and turns my life has taken. One thing I have come to realize is that I don't have enough time remaining to complete everything I have planned; thus a bucket list. Because of my lack of creativity, I copied one:

My Bucket List

1. buy a bucket
2. buy wine

3. fill the bucket with wine
4. drink bucket

That might work for a day or two, but then I would need to come up with a "to do" list for myself because that bucket list might be fun but not productive. It isn't like I want to die, but then I don't see myself living forever. The song by Kenny Chesney, "Everybody Wants to Go to Heaven," says it best with the lyrics that follow: "but nobody wants to go today." My path is clear; I know what I want to do and when the end does arrive, completed or not, I will be OK.

When it came time for me to retire from teaching, as I said before, I wrote a letter of resignation and got a job teaching at UW-SP for a year before finding a career in banking. When Raymond decided he no longer wanted to milk cows, he called Terry Brock. Terry is the guy that would take our cows to a dairy sale at Equity in Stratford. Before Terry was a "cattle jockey," he was a student at Marshfield Senior High while I was teaching there at the beginning of my career. He was in some of those earlier classes where the boys and girls were in separate groups. When Terry left our yard with the last load of cows on November 29, 2011, I took a picture of him for posterity. I wanted to take a picture of Raymond waving to his cows, but he said something like, "That is just stupid." I did get a picture of him sitting at the table filling out paperwork he was going to take to the auction for the sale of his cows. When Sarah told the boys that Grandpa Ray was selling his cows, their question was, "Is he going to sell his tractors?" No, his ten tractors are all here because we didn't sell the farm or the land; he is now a crop farmer. Luella told me years ago that her son, Raymond was most like his Uncle Charles Milz. Uncle Charles and his wife moved to town when they quit milking cows, and Charles died one year later. Raymond is outside every day, all four seasons of the year. Planting, harvesting, mowing the lawn, and making wood are just a few of the activities. There is more lawn mowed than when I was in charge and the wood he is making this year won't be used until 2020 or later. No, he doesn't want to sell any of it, before you even ask.

More than ten years ago I took a quilting class with my sister Pam and sister-in-law Karen; the quilt started in that class has yet to be completed. Not so with those two, they have their quilts completed, and I think Pam used hers as a wedding gift for a Meyer relative. I don't remember the name of the quilt, but it isn't an easy design; had to take a class to learn how to do it. Karen got me started with this hobby, and I enjoyed it for many years, but now I have to take action to complete several projects that have been started. After talking to Karen and Pam about finishing one of my quilts, with my plan to pay them, it is no longer my project. Another quilter friend of mine took one more quilt that was started by me so now I will have some outstanding bills to pay, but then, that is OK.

When I found an ad in the paper by Campus Quilts where they will make a quilt for you out of t-shirts, I knew how to complete another three quilts. About five years ago a friend of Sarah's, Jennifer Janus asked me to make a quilt for her using the t-shirts from the different marathons in which she had participated. After a person does 26.6 miles and earns a t-shirt it is hard to toss and after doing more than ten, how can a person wear all those shirts? I speak from experience because I did that once; ran a marathon. As I recall, Sarah talked me into it because I had been running half-marathons; "Run the first half and walk the second half," was her idea. We were planning a trip to Disney and got the idea to sign up for the runs and found the half-marathon was full but not the full marathon. So, after eight months of training, I ran my one and only marathon on January 11, 2009, with Sarah's younger sister, Laura Michel. I don't know if Laura still has her shirt but mine is gone because the shirt was white and I always manage to stain a white t-shirt. When I can't get the stain out, the garment has to go. But back to my projects, when Valerie saw what I had done for Jennifer, she wanted me to make one for her. I cut out the squares from the shirts that she gave me, which was as far as I got. WWW.campusquilt.com was the answer to my unfinished project for Valerie. Send the squares to them with a $100 deposit, and when completed they send the final bill, which once it is paid, you get your finished quilt. For Christmas of 2018, I plan to give Andrew and Parker each a quilt made from the outfits they wore when they were babies. Both of them wore a tiny tee that said: "If you think I am cute, you should see my Daddy." Outfits like that are hard to toss, or give away so Sarah gave me about thirty of them to make into quilts. I made one square for each of the boys which I put into a pillow. The rest of the clothing was washed, pressed, and sent to Campus Quilts. They turned out so lovely and now I can't see myself ever going back to making an entire quilt. Quilting, like training for a marathon takes over your life and neither activity is a high priority for me. For exercise, I wear a Fitbit and obsess daily about reaching ten thousand steps per day. Recently I read that if you do not life weights a person should at least wear a weight vest. So I ordered a weight vest with seventy pounds, and I wear it at least five times a week for 20 minutes. No, I don't use all seventy pounds; I am at 25 pounds so if you need weight for your vest, talk to me, I have extra.

C.S. Lewis said, "You can't go back and change the beginning, but you can start where you are and change the ending." At this point in my life, I am pleased with where I am. As a person I believe there is enough evidence to convict me of being Catholic if it were a crime, isn't it wonderful living in the United States where that is not true? Larry Lang, my brother-in-law says, "If you are born in the US, you have already won the lottery." As a wife, I am still in love with my husband, and we are still married. As a mother, I could not be more proud of my children. Both are good people, attend church, and contribute to society. As a teacher, I hope that each of my former students is better off because I did something to improve their life. As a banker, I know I dealt with people fairly. So now in my next thirty years; I want to take more time to write, but I would enjoy moving on to fiction. There is nothing natural about writing, but when recording what has happened in real life, everyone remembers it differently.

What I am going to do is call myself an author, but I do have issues that make it difficult. I found a book, <u>Writing the Blockbuster Novel</u> by Albert Zuckerman with an introduction by Ken Follett. In the introduction, Follett says an author needs to be imaginative, literate, and stubborn. Of those three qualities, my best is being stubborn and my worst is being imaginative. So going into this endeavor, I have found my strengths and weaknesses which should help. Follett says you can have all three qualities and still write a bad novel, but I want to try. He also explains that to write a person needs to give up things like movies, evenings at the pub with friends, TV shows, and chores around the house. Now I understand why authors have said they go away to a secluded place to write, but I know that isn't my style. Below I have other issues listed that work against me and my writing career.

In 2017 Joan Dickrell got me on the Board of the Friends of the Mead/McMillan which is only six miles from our farm. There are five meeting a year plus the annual meeting in January. During the year a person can volunteer to help by teaching classes when the school groups come to visit the center. It only took a year, and I found myself serving as secretary; there are so many people that work to make that place an excellent area for others to visit. Next year I might be moving on to being the treasurer, which could help me with another job I have.

As Clerk of the Town of Milladore, I need to learn how to use a spreadsheet to keep track of the revenues and expenditures for the town. The treasurer for the Mead has a spreadsheet set up for the Friends group so it will help me with the Clerk's job. I have been the Clerk since 2017, and I do plan to put my name on the ballot in 2019. No one is running against me, if anyone ever does, I will take my name off that year. The last Clerk, Richard Altman died in office, and I was told that might be the only way to get off the ballot.

Then there are the two book clubs I have joined in recent years which meet on the last Monday of the month in Marshfield at the Everett Roehl Public Library and the third Monday of the month in Mosinee at the Marathon County Public Library. At issue is the fact that I am more of a reader than a writer. I can recognize good writing. I say this because the book I voted for in the PBS one hundred best-loved books was the winner; To Kill A Mocking Bird. Not that I had read all of the books on the list, I never heard of the series that came in second, Outlander.

All of the above are just excuses, as a person ages, there are things we need to give up or think of as changing. While retiring was necessary, I do miss teaching. I no longer work full-time at the bank, I am on their Saturday schedule which means those that work 40-hours in a week work fewer Saturdays. When I taught CCD at St. Wenceslaus in Milladore, I asked my class to think about the idea of being

Christian. "If it were a crime to be Catholic, would there be enough evidence to convict you?" After some discussion about what evidence there would be for each of us, we wrote our obituary. What do you want people to say about you once you are gone? After teaching for thirty-four years, I had the opportunity to write a few to present as "examples" for my students. In my most recent obituary, I have listed a few things that are not completed at this time. The last sentence of that obituary is, "All her journals were completed, and her house was organized." Thus I have made a commitment; "Do not purchase another journal until all current ones are completed." It might take me thirty years to fill the journals I currently own.

Have you ever seen the following quote? "Today is the first day of the rest of your life." I found a quote from Frederick Buechner which states that idea in a better way. His quote follows: "In the entire history of the universe, let alone in your own history, there has never been another day just like today, and there will never be another just like it again. Today is the point to which all your yesterdays have been leading since the hour of your birth. It is the point from which all your tomorrows will proceed until the hour of your death. If you were aware of how precious today is, you could hardly live through it. Unless you are aware of how precious it is, you can hardly be said to be living at all." After finding this quote, I did some research on the author. He is an American writer and theologian who is an ordained Presbyterian minister. He has been writing for 60 years with some of his books being translated into many languages for publication around the world. Not sure I can compete with him, but that is OK.

Where is Raymond in all this and what are his plans for the future? I read someplace that a farmer always plans for a better year next year. That is Raymond, no worries because that is just the lack of faith in God and it could be worse. On our farm, no one worked harder than Raymond, and both of his children developed an excellent work ethic watching him as their example. Now he has joined the Romeo Breakfast Club at the Bunny Hop Restaurant in Junction City. The rules are:

1. No more than three people talking at once

2. One person must be listening at all times
3. We are retired and know everything and have all day to tell you
4. We don't have assigned seating but sit in the same seat anyway
5. Falling asleep at the table will not be tolerated
6. The waitress and cook are our friends
7. Your death is an acceptable excuse for missing breakfast
8. A change of clothes is required in case of spills and dribbles
9. No eating off someone else's plate
10. Wives are allowed but must sit outside

There is nothing else that can be said about this group except they do know how to have a good time and if you listen to them, they MIGHT have all the answers to the world's problems.

A few years ago I met Mike and Mary Gebert from Moon, Wisconsin. After I described where I was from Mike told me to tell Raymond "thank you" for buying the farm we currently own. He went on to explain his step-father; Donnie Hollar wanted to buy it but was out-bid by Raymond. Mike lived at home at the time, and he would have been responsible for helping with the milking if Donnie had purchased the place. Our farm had been sold by a woman after her husband died and while waiting for the sale, the Hollar family did the milking for the woman. Back in chapter three, I wrote that another man was bidding against Raymond but that individual offered the same price as Ray but also wanted three of the cows. This story can't be verified because both Donnie and his wife Virginia Hollar are gone, but I think we have solved the mystery of who was bidding against Raymond.

Just a few more thoughts before I say, "The End." I am "who I am" because of the people I have met during my life, and I wish I could write about each person. If you know me and are reading this book to find your name and wonder why I didn't tell our story; know that it isn't intentional, it might be a sheer loss of memory. Please let me know if you feel I forgot something so I can use the story

in my future writing as a fictional author. I can make the ending even better than the original.

Did you know that the word BIBLE is an acronym? It means "basic information before leaving earth." Again this is one of those notes I found someplace and feel it is worth sharing. Please pass it on to others.

With all of the above in mind, I am happy with my life, and if I don't get everything I have planned completed, it will be OK. I want to close this book with a prayer that I try to say every day.

"Prayer to St Michael the Archangel: Saint Michael the Archangel, defend us in battle. Be our defense against the wickedness and snares of the devil; may God rebuke him, we humbly pray; and do thou O Prince of the Heavenly Host, by the power of God, thrust into hell Satan and all the other evil spirits who prowl about the world seeking the ruin of souls. Amen."

OK

Printed in the United States
By Bookmasters